MW01051119

Thailand

Ting

Tong

Barry J Steel

Copyright © 2018 Barry J Steel

ISBN: 978-0-244-39229-1

All rights reserved, including the right to reproduce this book, or portions thereof in any form. No part of this text may be reproduced, transmitted, downloaded, decompiled, reverse engineered, or stored, in any form or introduced into any information storage and retrieval system, in any form or by any means, whether electronic or mechanical without the express written permission of the author.

Books by this author

Thailand After Divorce

Rigs, Pigs And Dirty Digs

Not For Children

Thailand Ting Tong

Favourable reviews for Barry's other grand works

"Rubbish - waste of money"

Debby

"Utter nonsense, one man's ravings passed off as a "book", gained nothing from reading this tripe, not even entertained! Please don't write another."

Anthony Rowland

"Sorry, but I found this book very unfunny. It might appeal to some, but to me it seemed full of offensive, juvenile language and attitudes."

Laura

"Well done, you have inspired me to write my memoirs. At least I've had some sort of useful life and can use punctuation. What a load of horseshit!"

Amazon Customer

Thanks for all the great comments. Please keep them coming.

BJ Steel

Barry's Special Message

When it comes to the subject of humour, in my humble opinion, there isn't a single topic on Earth which is off limits. If certain, very boring, members of society tell you that you aren't allowed to laugh at something then it is your duty as an individual to laugh twice as hard. If you find that you feel guilty after sniggering at something inappropriate then don't worry, that is a beautiful thing...it means that you have both a sense of humour and a conscience.

If you disagree with the above statement then please don't read this book...I can promise that I don't hold back!

With thanks to Grindon Loop and also my ex-wife. Without her heinous actions I never would've been able to write this book.

Contents

PART THREE

I Think I Quite Like It Here

PART ONE

A Homeless Man Is Better Than A Dead One

Chapter One

Let's Have A Catch Up Shall We?

I want to start by thanking you for purchasing this book. Or maybe you've found this in some strangers bin? The latter would be quite shameful for the both of us. Either way thank you for sparing me some of your precious time. I want you to sit back and relax now, get comfy, maybe even pour yourself a nice glass of lukewarm milk. For the next couple of hours Uncle Barry is going to look after you. If you're starting to feel like you're being groomed at this point then I promise that isn't my intention at all.

I'm going to surmise that you have read my first book Thailand After Divorce but not the follow up book Not For Children? I say this because hardly anyone bought the latter book. Maybe it was a bit too politically incorrect, maybe it was because it didn't have Thailand in the title, or maybe it was just a big pile of smelly shit? I tell myself the reason is it's just a tad too extreme for most people and as I rely on word of mouth for my books to sell, maybe that book was akin to someone recommending a good snuff film. By the way have you noticed that book goes by two different titles depending on which format you buy? There's a really, really interesting story behind that. Moving on now, I've decided to write this very brief bridging chapter, it basically means you won't have to bother reading the middle book.

Thailand After Divorce ended in July 2014 and it ended with me feeling disillusioned with Pattaya and wanting to see the rest of the world. Therefore you may be surprised to learn that I actually returned there three months later in the October. This was due to some horrendous bad luck I had in the same week that Thailand After Divorce was published and I felt a need to escape from it all. In fact all three times that I've released a book I've had bad luck immediately afterwards. I'm really hoping this time it's a case of that ancient and famous saying,

The fourth time you release a book you don't have a spell of bad luck in the immediate aftermath

The holiday in October, my fifth time there, was almost on a par with my very first trip to Pattaya. This was mainly due to the company of a hilarious bald man from Australia called Greg. When I returned to England I was unemployed for quite a long time. When I eventually had money again I returned to Pattaya for a sixth time in June 2015. That holiday was enjoyable but peppered with bad luck from start to finish. At the end of it I was sat in Bangkok airport departure lounge and I was just as miserable as the rest of the people in that God awful place. If someone had approached me at the time and told me it would be nearly two and half years before I was to go back to Thailand I probably would have quietly stood up, walked to the toilets in a dignified manner and then slit my own throat.

Not For Children ended on a high note of me getting back into the offshore industry after eight months away from it. In real life though there was no high note at all. As expected when that book was published the bad luck kicked in straight away, in the next nine months I only worked two weeks! When I look back now I honestly don't know how I survived it.

That is pretty much you now up to date, there's obviously lot more material in that other book but I really can't be bothered to type it all out again. Nineteen months of my life summed up in only a handful of paragraphs. How incredibly dull I must be.

Chapter Two

Hell Hath No Fury Like A Complete Bitch

March 2016, life was grim, the oil crisis seemed to have affected every sector of heavy industry. I was living out of my overdraft which I'd extended to the maximum amount I could get. It's during times of unemployment when you find out just how evil an ex-wife can be. It still puzzles me to this day how a divorce that was initially amicable has gotten worse over the years rather than better. Someone who was once your best friend has now grown into something of an arch nemesis. All I've ever wanted was to be left alone to get on with my life but I've had no such luck. Her need to have a grip of control over me has caused nothing but problems.

In the final week of March she was on her period and it must have been a bad one because at the start of the week she committed an act of unspeakable evil. I was just getting over the shock of it when she decided to go for a double whammy, four days later committing another act of pure evil that surpassed the first one. In my opinion a hormonal, bleeding woman shouldn't be allowed to make any decisions for that one week of the month. They're nothing but a danger to themselves and the people around them. Her monthly psychosis should've had absolutely nothing more to do with me the day we broke up. But here we were more than three and a half years after the fact and in this condition she was making decisions that were designed to ruin my life.

I was left with my head firmly up my arse. I decided to do what I always do when I've got a headache and went for a walk in the countryside. At the start of this walk I was down in the dumps and had a sinking feeling of being backed into a corner. By the end of the walk I had a smile on my face and a feeling of a huge weight being taken off my back. In this short time I had concocted a plan that was almost bullet proof, some might say borderline evil. It's worth pointing out that this initial plan I devised was much more extreme than what I actually ended up doing. The original idea was just to move to Thailand as at that point in life I felt that I had no reason to stay in England anymore. Over the following weeks as the shock of her actions subsided a bit the plan evolved. It actually went through four incarnations altogether but each of those plans had one common link connecting them…I had to sell my house!

Please forgive me for these incredibly short chapters so far, I promise that they do start getting a little bit longer. Put it down to me being a bit rusty at this hobby of mine and also I didn't really want to waste too much ink on that cunt.

Chapter Three

The Evil Plan

If divorce taught me one thing it's that a person can change their life whenever they want to. It just takes a little bit of balls is all. Life isn't like a soap opera that you watch on the telly, where a character makes a big decision and then they're inevitably sat in the back of a taxi all teary eyed, never to be seen or heard from again. If you want to make a change then just go ahead and do it, if you find out that you don't like the change then either change it back or change it for something else again. We're only here once and its pointless putting things off into a future that you might not even get.

For a very long time now I've had this little dream about buying a motorhome and touring Britain in it. It was on my list of things I'd do if I ever won the lottery, which obviously means it was something I'd never end up doing. During one of my long spells on the dole there was a point where I got worried about not being able to pay my mortgage anymore. I'd already lost one house in my divorce and at the time I thought to myself,

If I lose another house I'll just buy a motorhome and fulfil that little dream of mine.

That one little thought took away most of the stress I was feeling in one fell swoop. If the worst thing that could happen in my life was that I'd live in a motorhome then what was the point of worrying about anything at all? (Maybe that thought sounds horrifying to you?)

So as my little evil plan evolved the motorhome idea came back to me and then it became centre stage. Right now you might be wondering if you could live in a van? Well I'll admit from the outset that I definitely *couldn't* live in one all year round, but that would never happen anyway. When I'm employed I have to live at work. I'm given my own bed, shower and toilet, my clothes are washed for me and my meals are prepared by a chef. An oil rig would seem like luxury once I'd moved into a van. As for the unemployment I'd been suffering, oil prices were now back on the rise and phone calls for jobs were creeping up steadily. If another oil crash happens it means I could just drive down south and find work in a fabshop. It's not feasible for me to take these low paid jobs whilst having a mortgage because they don't pay any dig (accommodation) money. If I lived in a van who needs dig money?! Another huge factor in devising this plan was the fact that my parents had just decided to start living in Europe during summer. This is something they're able to do from working hard all their lives and being complete mingebag's with their money (when I was young I would have to go to school with the fronts of shoes glued because they didn't want to buy me a new pair. Twats!) So for four months each year their house is sat empty. And of course there is the piece de resistance...Pattaya! If I decided to live like a filthy scumbag gypo then I would basically be living with hardly any bills at all! This would enable me to fulfil another goal of mine, to live abroad in the winter. When those clocks go back in October, jump on a plane and don't return until they go forward again at the end of March. A full five months in Pattaya each year! (Or somewhere else if I ever get bored of the place). All in all on average in a good year I'd only be spending around three months in the motorhome and even then my parent's house would probably be empty for me to use if I wished so.

April 2016, I'd just turned 35 and I had a new life plan. There was just one little snag with it at this point, the repossessed house I'd bought in 2013 still wasn't finished yet. The entire downstairs of the house was still the same as the day I'd bought it. This was due to me spending most of my money on holidays when I was working and then not being able to afford to do it up when I was out of work. I'll give you some advice that I learned the hard way, when buying a house make sure you get the front room done first!

I was faced with a heart-breaking and undeniable truth…I could *not* return to Pattaya until my house was both finished and sold. In other words I had absolutely no idea when I'd be able to return to my true home again. That thought is soul destroying and if you're a Pattaya addict then you'll understand exactly how I felt.

I must admit that the longer a person is away from Pattaya the easier it gets over time. It's still always there in the back of your mind but it eventually becomes a more distant thought. This brings to mind two conversations I had with two separate men that I met on two separate oil rigs. Both these conversations were virtually identical. These men were ex-Pattaya addicts and their own stories of Pattaya were the same as mine. They would go there as often as they could and on the return home they would suffer from the Pattaya Blues, with the city constantly on their minds. What set these men apart from most I meet is that they had stopped going there years before but they were still single. When I said,
    'You should go back'
Their reactions were the same. A face of deep thought and almost a look of a shudder passing through their body. The reply from each of them was,
    'No'
I can only assume that their addictions to the place must have been extreme and they felt better off

without Pattaya in their lives. I suppose me asking that was akin to me asking a reformed smackhead if he wanted to try a little bit of heroin again. For me personally my own addiction to the place is one I thoroughly enjoy. It's a complete step out of reality and as long as you're able to keep returning to reality afterwards then it shouldn't be a problem. That being said, I knew I had to stay away from the place because returning would've only kick started my addiction again and delayed my big plan.

I'm going to tell you a story now that is completely irrelevant to this book but I do get humiliated in it so it's worth including. As I was cracking on doing up my house to get it sold a mate of mine was doing up a house for him to live in. One day we both went out to a retail park together and at one point we ended up in a furniture shop. We were just about to leave when an annoying salesman approached us. He had a chubby tongue which gave him a stupid sounding voice, hence making him even more annoying. We politely told him we didn't need assistance and that we were leaving. This is the point where he should've just walked away and admittedly this is what he initially did start to do but after only a couple of steps he stopped in his tracks, turned around and felt the need to ask us this,

'Which one is dragging the other one round kicking and screaming then?'

I was absolutely mortified! At what point in our society did it become normal to assume that two male acquaintances were homosexuals?! I know what you might be thinking right now,

But Barry, you have actually fucked men

That may be true but it's beside the point and in my defence all the men I've shagged have looked remarkably like women. (If this is your first time reading one of my books you will very quickly realise that I am a deeply flawed individual) After he asked us this I said something to let him know of my distaste for him and then stormed out of the shop. When my mate walked out he had a big grin on his face, he seemed flattered by it all. What bothered me the most is that my mate is bigger than me, it's obvious who the bitch would've been if we had been a pair of benders. If that spastic salesman had thought it then how many other people that day had thought it as well? Had every passing person conjured up an image of me biting a pillow in glorious agony?! That thought left my blood running cold!

Back to the main story now, please forgive me if I get a bit side tracked throughout this book.

So my plan was in place, I was back in work and I was on a mission to get my house finished and put on the market. But as with all my plans I was to quickly hit a stumbling block.

Chapter Four

What Devilry Is This?

In late spring 2016 I finally landed what I thought would be a steady job. Unfortunately in the summer of that year I suffered my first semi-serious accident at work, at the hands of a complete mong. Not serious enough to cause any lasting damage but serious enough for a doctor to send me home and tell me to spend a week lying down. It was the last thing I needed, in my industry sick pay is virtually non-existent. I was losing both money and time working on the house, although this setback became a very minor issue compared to what happened next.

On my fifth day on the settee I started to get cabin fever, I was completely bored out of my skull. For some reason crack cocaine entered my head. It had been years since I'd touched the stuff and even back then it was something I did only very rarely. Once I get an idea in my head it's very hard for me to get it back out of there. Still to this day I'm searching for that 'Off Button' for my stupid little brain, I don't think I'm ever going to find it though. Needless to say a couple of hours later I was driving around in my car against the doctor's orders. I don't possess any phone numbers for drug dealers so I was out in search of a hooker to make my purchase for me. Picking up a hooker is a very easy thing to do in Teesside as we boast three red-light districts. Prostitution here is as natural as finding a shopping trolley in a beck. It didn't take me long to find a respectable lady who would do my shopping for me. Once the rocks were in hand I decided as an added bonus to bring her back to mine. My restricted mobility meant sex was off the cards but a man is never too poorly to receive a blowjob. It was whilst driving the pair of us home she asked me a question which was to have quite a big impact on me,

'Have you ever had a blowjob when you've been doin' a pipe?'

'No'

'Well do you want to try it? Most men seem to like it'

'Aye'

When I think back now I'm fairly certain that this lady had an ulterior motive for asking me this.

If you've never had crack before then it's basically crystalized cocaine. Most people wrongly believe it's a harder drug than coke but it's actually exactly the same only you smoke it instead of snorting it. Crystallising it makes it purer and smoking it makes the effect from it stronger. You get an instant euphoric feeling that makes you sink into your seat but the high doesn't last long and as soon as it wears off you immediately want it again. When you run out of it altogether it makes you almost suicidal. Although it's not physically addictive the mental addiction is enormous for some people, this is why the drug has a reputation for wrecking lives. As I've already mentioned, it was something I could take or leave in my younger days.

So I get her back to mine and before too long I'm sat down with my trousers around my ankles with my tiddle in her mouth and a crackpipe in my hand. Once I was suitably stiff I burned the crack, inhaled and moments later exhaled. As soon as the euphoria kicked in I made a new discovery! Crack makes your testicles and bellend ultra-sensitive! The mixture of a crack hit and sloppy sensitive blowjob was the most amazing sensation that I've ever had in my life. I suggest to you that you *never ever* try it! Some experiences in life are best left well alone. Two days later I didn't know how many rocks we'd been through or how many blowjobs that poor woman had given me. I just knew I was skint again and badly needed some sleep. At least I'd followed the doctors' orders of staying on the settee for a week.

If you're assuming that this new experience became a problem for me then you would be correct. Sitting here now writing this I can admit something that I couldn't admit to my mates at the time and that's that I became a full blown crack monster. I could go to work fine and not be bothered because I knew getting hold of crack in the North Sea was an impossibility.

Once I was home though and it was readily available again then I was out of control. The unemployment I'd endured in the last two years had left my life completely devoid of fun. The only thing that had occupied my time was family induced stress. Now I had money again I was using it all blindly for self-gratification. I would have the majority of two weeks getting completely fucked and then I would dust myself off and step back out into society like a respectable human being.

I was to quickly learn that lots of hookers knew about this little trick and I ended up being on first name terms with quite a few of Teesside's suppliers of pleasure. There was one time when a girl persuaded me to let her mate come along with us. Admittedly inviting two thieves into my house wasn't very appealing but I agreed anyway. Just when I thought I'd discovered the ultimate experience it turned out that there was an even better one. I'll let you use your imagination as to what I had them doing. If you are a person who is completely devoid of imagination then I'll give you a clue…I *didn't* have them hoovering my carpet and washing the dishes.

This wonderful affliction of mine became so bad that on Christmas Day 2016 whilst everyone else was enjoying a family dinner, I was sat in my front room with a hooker smoking crack. I think it was around this point when I realised I'd developed a bit of a problem. (A special mention to the man somewhere in the UK who bought a copy of Thailand After Divorce on Christmas Day 2016. My heart bled for you when I noticed that sale. You must have had even bigger problems than me at the time!)

I'll put your mind at ease now as I do not want you getting concerned about me. I eventually got a grip of myself and ploughed back into getting the house finished. That little habit of mine was merely a delay in my plan and I have to admit that I don't regret any of it at all.

Chapter Five

A Very Tedious Chapter Indeed

After what you've read so far I don't want to mislead you into thinking that I have any sort of an interesting life. I'm as dull, uninteresting and boring as the next man on the street. This chapter will prove that.

It was early spring 2017 when my house was finally finished and put up for sale. I had done all I could do with my plan and now I just had to sit and wait. It would take nearly eight months to sell and I didn't get a single offer in that entire time! (Not including the offer from the people who actually bought the house of course)

At first I was initially hopeful with the sudden rush of viewings I had but I quickly realised that these people were those twisted perverts who have a fetish for looking at other people's houses without any intention of buying them! Some people appal me! By the time I finally did get an offer I was that fed up I accepted nearly 10% lower than the original asking price.

For those eight months my life was completely on hold and I felt like I was living in the doldrums. For a man like me, who generally dislikes human beings, it was a hard pill to swallow knowing that my destiny lay in the hands of some total stranger.

That time wasn't completely unproductive though, I managed to bank enough money for a three month holiday in Pattaya and I also got to pick out which motorhome I wanted to buy. It's fair to say that I became a bit obsessed with motorhomes during those months. I looked on helpful forums, reading the comments written by incredibly straitlaced people whose attempts at humour left me both bewildered and confused. YouTube was another good source for material and tips. I could happily sit for an hour at a time watching videos of the beautiful Scottish Highlands taken by dash cams.

At work I was jumping from rig to rig, meeting new people and telling them about my evil plan. Most men told me that they wouldn't think twice about it if they were single. I'd meet the occasional bloke who would be bemused and perplexed by the idea of it all. I would be asked how I would be able to afford to retire if I was only working half the year and then blowing all my earnings in Thailand. Overtime I perfected the answer to this question,

'Any man who plans ahead thirty years into the future is an imbecile who is destined to die young'

It's worth noting at this point that I'm a strange person and I do genuinely say strange things. In general people told me to go for it. I would explain to people that just because I'm doing this now it doesn't mean its forever. If I find that lifestyle isn't for me I'd just flog the motorhome

One thing you have to do when you decide you're going to live in a van is what clutter you're going to keep and what you can get rid of. Luckily I'm not the type to get attached to material stuff. I'm not a materialistic person at all, in fact I'm an advertiser's worst nightmare. The only advert I can recall seeing on the telly and then made a point of going out to buy the product was Branston Baked Beans....I was deeply dissatisfied and never bought them again.

We live in an age where it's easy to sell things online. I'm a technophobe and I'm also incredibly lazy so I didn't bother trying to sell anything, I just gave it all to my destitute older brother. He promptly took it all to a pawn shop and the dick never did tell me how much he made from it all. Afterwards it turned out that my entire existence could fit into four small cardboard boxes and two medium sized suitcases. This was still far too much for a motorhome but I suppose that's why our parents have lofts. My mind became so motorhome based that one night when I was incredibly drunk, I was stumbling up the stairs to go and have a piss in the toilet and I actually said out loud to myself,

'I could do without these fucking stairs'

It was also during those months when I started having a recurring memory from when I was 17. I'd just quit sixth form college after ten months attendance and I was sitting at the dining room table nervously telling my parents what I'd done. At one point in the conversation one of them asked me what I wanted to do with my life and I can remember saying,

'I don't know, I just don't want to end up being a robot'

I kept thinking of this moment because it's my earliest memory of knowing that I didn't want the same type of life as everyone else. The truth is I did the exact opposite of what I'd said. Soon after I started an apprenticeship and then I conformed to society like everyone else. I hated my job, I hated paying bills and life was a big ball of stress. Even after my divorce I still had this inbuilt need in me to conform. After renting a flat for a year my only desire was to get another mortgage and burden myself with debt again. This is what society drums into us from school age,

Be a little turning cog in this big dreary machine
We're all different but at the same time we're all conditioned to be the same. I'm reminded of a little moment I had in November 2016. I was on a train heading to Aberdeen and I was on the part of the line that runs along the south coast of Fife in Scotland. It's a beautiful stretch of line and you can look across the Forth of Fife and see Edinburgh in the distance. This

day was sunny but freezing cold due to a strong wind. As the train passed a beach I noticed a fully grown man standing on it wearing a pair of shorts and flying a big kite. He was there on his own. Probably anyone else sat on that train who noticed him just thought to themselves, *what a buffoon* and then quickly took no notice of him. But I didn't. I stared at him for as long as the window would allow and then I went into deep thought. He was clearly doing something that he loved and the opinions of other people wouldn't have mattered to him at all, no matter how strange it seemed. For me personally on a cold winters day the last thing that would enter my head is leaving the house half naked to play a kids game. You never know, maybe that man was stood there with his big gay kite thinking to himself,

I'm so glad that I'm not sitting in a half-finished house right now with drugs and hookers

The point that I'm struggling to make here is that we're all different and in life you have to go out and do whatever makes you happy regardless of the opinions of other people.

That man didn't realise that there was a hack 'author' creepily staring at him from a train window and that his little hobby would get him a mention in a book. He'll die without ever even knowing that he's in this book. I suppose that means it doesn't make a blind bit of difference to him.

Chapter Six

Finally Off The Goddamn Grid

When I received the offer on the house everything became real then. If my house had sold quickly then maybe I would've had feelings of hesitation and panic but I can tell you that after nearly seven months of waiting the only feelings I felt were relief and excitement. It meant I could go straight back to Thailand! Any nervousness about moving into a big car would be dealt with after my holiday.

After I received the offer I drove straight down to the disastrous city of Hull. It's a place that should be avoided by *everyone* but unfortunately it's the closest location to me of a Thai Consulate. I was in need of a tourist visa for my long stint away. When I arrived I felt disappointment when I saw the nondescript building in the middle of a trading estate. The disappointment grew even more when I entered the building and realised all the staff were from Yorkshire! I'd been dusting off my very limited Thai out loud on the drive down. The only Asian women I saw were a couple of Thai brides sitting in the waiting area with their husbands.

The wait for my visa was only around twenty minutes and during this time I was kept entertained by the very abrupt Yorkshireman who works there. He reminded me of Basil Fawlty with the way he spoke to people. Some poor chap came wandering in and approached him,

'I'd like some advice on marrying in Thailand please?'

'You've come to the wrong place'

I had to stifle a giggle at this point. This poor bloke didn't even have a Yorkshire accent, maybe he lived local or maybe he'd had quite a long drive to be delivered this sound advice. To be honest I didn't really feel that much pity for him. I don't want to sound cruel here but my God he was ugly. I very much doubt that marriage would've been 'true love'. To me he was the personification of nonsense.

After the short wait I was handed back my passport with the beautiful shiny visa inside of it. What a wonderful feeling that was, I drove back home with a smile on my face. My annual trip to that place is going to be something that I always look forward to, even if it is in smelly Hull. I really hope that Yorkshireman never gets the sack, it'll be a treat watching him again.

I made a conservative guess as to when the sale of my house would go through. I knew it wasn't going to take long because my solicitor is a family friend. It's unbelievable how quickly these money grabbers can do their jobs when you actually know them. Using my guesstimate I booked a hotel that I'd used twice before on Soi 7. I only booked 60 nights there, for the final month of my stay I would have to extend my visa again whilst I was out there. I was also pretty certain that after 60 days on Soi 7 I would be quite desperate to stay in a quieter part of the city for the final part of my holiday. Again this was something that I could sort out when I was already there. Once the hotel was booked I then booked my flights as well.

Before the house sale was finalised I went and worked one final trip of the year offshore. The excitement I felt during this trip was almost tangible. Each night I would lay in my cot fantasising. A flood of Pattaya memories came rushing back to me, things that I had completely forgotten about. I suppose a psychologist would call these suppressed memories. Not suppressed because they were bad but supressed for being too good! When Pattaya is off the cards in your life then you need to put all the thoughts of the place into a little storage box and keep it right at the back of your brain, otherwise you'll end up torturing yourself. On that trip offshore I also allowed myself to listen to some albums I hadn't heard in years. I reserve them for Pattaya Beach and hotel balconies, listening to them in England is only frustrating for me. Although I was confined to a big floating prison in the middle of the sea, that was still a happy little time for me. Pure excitement.

When the house sold I had to move into my parent's house. Luckily for all three of us they were on holiday at the time. I was only there for ten days before I went on holiday so my prediction for the sale and dates for the holiday had been more or less spot on.

During this little spell at my parent's house I went on that same walk where my plan had been conceived. I didn't do this for any profound reasons, it's just a regular walk of mine. At the point of the walk where I'd had my little light bulb moment I actually let out a chuckle followed by a grin. It was a mixture of joy and relief. It had taken nearly twenty months but now it had finally happened! I'd done that walk so many times during that time with a feeling of uncertainty and frustration.

The day you get to delete nearly all of your direct debits is a very good day believe me. What was left of my monthly bills could now be paid in less than one day's earnings. I went out and did a shop in Tesco and didn't even look at the prices of anything I bought. I think I may possibly have been the happiest homeless man on the planet.

I can't say that I made a *lot* of money from my house but I suppose I could describe it as a tidy sum. I had absolutely no intention of buying a motorhome until after my holiday but at the same time I didn't want this money sitting in my bank account. Any man who goes to Pattaya with a large amount in the bank is a complete fool. So many men have gone there and blown every penny they had. It's one thing to come back from Thailand skint but to come back both skint and homeless, well that sounds very much like hitting rock bottom to me. Therefore I basically had to hide all that money from myself. It was put in a place that would be impossible for me to get my grubby little hands on it whilst I was away.

By the way, you *might* be pleased to hear that my ex threw a monumental tantrum when she found out what I'd done. What a silly sausage she is.

Chapter Seven

The Pedestal Bin

Have you ever read a book where the author has had a deep discussion about a pedestal bin? No, neither have I. For you though that is about to change.

In the month of May 2014 I finally completed the posh bathroom in my house. To give it a special finish I went out and bought a lovely little pedestal bin for it. It was smooth and round, made of stainless steel, about ten inches high and six inches across. The lever on it was an absolute pleasure to use. After I placed the bin in a perfect spot for it I had to go out and buy the correct sized bin bags. If memory serves me well these little bags came in a roll of five hundred and the roll was around three inches thick. Because I lived alone and didn't really make much mess in my bathroom it meant this poor little bin was rarely used. I'd say on average I would only have to change the bag three times a year.

It was during the summer of 2017 when the little bin was getting one of its rare bag change outs (I'm sure it used to smile at me whenever I did this) I took the roll of bags from the cupboard under the sink and whilst I was tearing a new one off I noticed the size of the roll in my hand. It was pretty much the same thickness as the day I'd bought it three years earlier. With this realisation came a thought,

I won't live long enough to use these up!

That thought showed me just how short our lives really are. We can measure life in seasons, years and even rolls of bin bags.

There are some people who describe life as a game. If you take a step back from your existence, look at it, ponder on it and truly see it as a game then afterwards you quickly realise that it's always worth taking risks. You should never ever be scared of taking these risks, no matter what they are. Some other people come out with the line,

Live each day as if it's your last

The people who say this are complete bellend's! It's an impossibility to live that way. I prefer,

Live each year as if it's your last

If you were told you only had one more year left to live what would you like to do in that time? If you find that you end up with a long list of things you would like to do then I suggest you go out and do as many as possible whilst you've still got breath in your lungs. So many people out there think to themselves,

I'll do that when I'm older

Old age isn't a guarantee for anyone. Everyone knows someone else who has died just before or just after retirement age. That could quite easily happen to you or me. (Preferably you rather than me)

When I'm drunk I have a habit of coming out with mildly 'profound' statements and philosophies. Admittedly I doubt that any of them have been truly original. The next day I've inevitably forgotten everything I said the night before so these statements are lost in time. Probably for the better. Here's a couple that I have actually remembered, you can feel free to use them if you wish,

When you're young you worry about debt, when you're old you worry about death

In life we are all standing in a queue and at the end of it is a coffin. You can stand in this queue staring at the floor and shuffling your feet or you can stand there banging a drum

I was working away one time and I was in a pub with a work mate, we were both inebriated. I'd just come up another little gay philosophy and I decided to tell him it.

'What it is mate…is that no matter what I do with my life, no matter how hard I try, I'm going to be dead at the end of it and there's nothing I can do about it. So if I'm destined to be dead then what's the point of me worrying about anything at all? Everything else seems minor compared to that.'

I sat waiting for a nod of recognition from him. Instead I got this reply,

'That's just a longer way of saying, *you're a long time dead!*'

I don't see the similarity!

You may have noticed that all my little philosophies revolve around death? You may also be thinking to yourself right now,

Who the fuck is this divorced, homeless, drug addict who's trying to give me life advice?!

Please don't think that I'm trying to persuade you into selling your house and buying a motorhome, only a complete idiot would do such a thing. I'm merely letting you into my mind so you can get a better understanding of how my stupid brain works.

On the day I moved out of my house the shiny little pedestal bin was one of the items I left behind for the new owners. I did actually pick up the roll of bags, it was my intention to keep them to see if my prediction would come true. In the end though I placed them back in the cupboard and left them…I didn't really see the point.

Part Two

An Incurable Addiction To Perversion

Chapter Eight

A Brief Word Of Warning

In the year 2016 my granddad had to have one of his legs amputated, the poor old bastard. The night before the operation me and my dad went to visit him in the hospital. As we were walking through the hospital my dad said to me,

'Remind me not to buy him a pair of socks for Christmas'

Just before I flew out to Pattaya I went to visit my granddad in the care home and I said to him,

'Granddad, I'm off to Thailand for three months, whatever you do, don't die while I'm away 'cos it'll spoil my holiday. When I get back you can do whatever you want.'

I said this to him with my nana sitting there. If you think that sounds nasty then don't worry, my granddad was far more brutal than me in his day. Luckily for me he can barely argue back now.

This is the type of humour I've grown up with and spent my entire life around. I'm telling you this because so far I've kept this book very child friendly but now it's time to ramp things up a few gears.

Looking back to my first book it seems so tame, with my second book I introduced political incorrectness but I always felt the need to explain beforehand why it was ok to say such things. With my third book I didn't care and just wrote whatever I wanted without feeling the need to explain why it wasn't bad to say such things. However I have to admit that when I finished my last book I did read a couple of bits and thought to myself

I might have gone a bit too far there

So I did actually tone some of it down slightly. However there's a good chance that this will be my final book so I'm just going to write whatever I want and I really don't give a fuck about offending anyone at all.

Whenever I meet people and I feel comfortable in their company I will always try my best to shock them. The usual response is a chuckle, a shake of the head and then a shrug of the shoulders. To me being offensive is as natural as a black moaning about being hard-done by.

If you found that last line offensive then you may want to reconsider reading on. It's going to get a lot worse than that.

Chapter Nine

It Looks Like Pattaya, It Smells Like Pattaya...By Jove! It *Is* Pattaya!

On the way to the airport the taxi ran into a blizzard, I remember thinking,

Good I hope it stays like this for the next three months

When I finally made it to the airport I sat at the bar and text as many people as I knew to rub their noses in the fact I was going to Pattaya for three months. In hindsight I may have jinxed myself because that blizzard became an omen to an absolutely horrendous journey. From my door to the hotel took over 26 hours! A journey which normally takes a maximum of 22 hours.

I had thought about writing about that journey but then I realised it was completely boring so I'm not bothering. The only part worth mentioning was my Thai taxi driver who referred to himself as Mr Tango. Although I felt emotionally exhausted from the travelling, as we pulled onto Beach Road I let out a big grin. Mr Tango grinned along with me. In that moment I felt really happy and gay, full of zest and spunk.

I'd went on this holiday knowing there were to be no half measures, I wasn't there to fuck about. (Actually that's exactly why I was there but just not in that sense of the phrase). Before I walked into the hotel I went into the 7/11 and bought a 35cl bottle of Sangsom (Thai whisky...sort of).

After unpacking my case I went and sat on my balcony to soak up the glorious view and enjoy a couple of glasses of whisky. In past holidays I'd mixed coke with this stuff but I've since grown fond of drinking it neat like I would a proper Scotch.

The view from the balcony was spectacular, it's a sea view overlooking Soi 7 and you can see the south coast of Pattaya all the way up to the high rises in the north. Plus my favourite part, the island of Koh Lan. After enjoying a nice juicy cigarette I then called reception and ordered an in-room happy ending massage. In past holidays I'd had a couple of bad experiences where a happy ending wasn't offered. My English prudishness had sometimes prevented me from telling the receptionist exactly what I wanted. Here I was now with absolutely no shame and very little dignity.

'I'd like an oily massage please. Happy ending'

I'd gone away this trip looking my best and it's with some regret that I have to inform you that my disgusting ego was inflated even further this night. I decided to bring myself back down to reality by going short time twice and finishing the night with a long time. And yes, both the short times were with blokes. I needed to get that out of my system straight away. (I'd been masturbating over ladyboy porn quite profusely in the run up to the holiday). The joy of spuffing into a ladyboy's mouth is an experience I shall never tire of. The long time was with a real woman and I have to admit it became quite laborious. Bearing in mind I'd already shot my muck before I'd even left the hotel then it left very little chance of being able to cum again for a fourth time. If I had managed to climax no doubt it would've been nothing more than a squeak of thin air, after all I'm not a machine, I'm just a man…flesh and blood. Still, the blowjob on the balcony during a fag break was a nice touch.

Earlier that night I'd had a chat with a woman who I'd met two and half years previously. At that time she'd been fairly new to Pattaya, quite shy and reserved. She could barely speak English so I'd sat her on my balcony to settle her down and we used a Thai/English translator app on her phone to speak. I'm not sure what that app did to my rubbish jokes but it seemed to make them even funnier than watching a hard-left feminist being gang-raped by a group of Somalian refugees. I had her in a fit of giggles.

Here we were now in December 2017, she had bleached blonde hair, a boob job, she could speak

English and she was sitting there very, very drunk. The transformation was unbelievable and it wasn't a good one either. She's a good looking woman but I didn't barfine her, I actually walked out of that bar feeling quite sad. The way Pattaya changes people is never in a good way. The first time I met her she would've made a good wife, for anyone who's into that type of thing, but seeing her again I knew she would never marry or if she did it would be brief. That bar was now her life and her life was only destined to get worse. I'm not preaching here by the way, it's because of men like me that these women end up like this. We shag them and leave them the next day. They go through this night after night and some of the men out there are right evil bastards. How can that life not affect a person's mind?

My second night would turn out to be my night of 'dark pleasures'. I was on Walking Street and I decided to pay a visit to the Negroid bar. A chocolate woman quickly caught my eye so I took her to a back room for short time. It was the shittest shag I'd ever had in that city! There was nothing scatological about it, it was just shit! A blowjob with a condom?! Maybe in some back street of Middlesbrough but not blummin Pattaya!

I left that room feeling quite frustrated and then found myself in a nightclub. I spotted another black woman, she had a shaved head and an athletic body. I needed to restore my faith in darkie's so I took her back to my hotel. She was Ugandan and on my balcony I had one of the most interesting conversations I've ever had in that city. Ugandan women always seem to have an intelligence and life experience beyond most. I'm not just saying this to counter balance any racial humour in this book, it's the truth. I've never met a Ugandan woman yet whose company I haven't enjoyed. She was brilliant in bed as well. God bless niggers!

Chapter Ten

Insanity Is An Illusion

On my third day I decided that I'd either descended from a Greek God or I had turned completely insane. When this city gets a grip on you, it does so in a massive way. After another happy ending massage it now meant seven different people had done rude things to me. My budget would just not allow for this sort of despicable behaviour!

The English translation for the title of this book is 'Thailand Crazy'. If you've never been to Pattaya then you really can't comprehend what an insane place it is. I know that many people have written books about Thailand and Pattaya in particular, I've never read any of them so I don't know how well other authors have managed to capture the insanity of the place. (No doubt most of them have done a far better job than me) I know that no mere mortal will ever truly capture the essence of Pattaya on paper but I'm going to give it my best shot.

When you walk around this city there are many rock bands and one song in particular you are guaranteed to hear each night is Hotel California by The Eagles. If you've never heard this song then you either live in a jungle or Northern Iraq, where the only form of entertainment is raping goats. The reason I want to mention this song is because I've came up with my own theory about why it's so popular there. The song is a metaphor for Hollywood excess and the comparison to Pattaya is obvious. There's one line in the song in particular which always strikes a chord with me

We are all prisoners here, of our own device

Any Pattaya addict reading that line will instantly know what I'm talking about. The city sucks you in and trust me there are many, many men out there who truly are trapped there. Some even living on the streets! It is a true addiction and the trick is managing to stay on top of it.

There was a night much later on in the holiday where I got talking to a bar owner from Teesside. We briefly asked each other which towns we were from and then I asked him how long he'd lived out there. The answer was either seven or nine years, I forget which. I said to him,

'Can I ask you a question mate?'

'Anything you like.'

'What does it do to your head living out here?'

'It completely fucks it mate. It makes you mental'

'Do you ever think about going back to Teesside?'

'Quite a lot, but I never will'

The briefest of chats which encapsulates Pattaya perfectly. I've fantasised about buying a property in

Pattaya ever since my first trip there. There was even a time that I was in contact with an estate agent asking about flats. By the time this holiday was over I knew it will be something that I will never do. If I lived out there I would die young, plain and simple. Also when I'm out there I love it, I don't think I'd say the same if I lived there though. The magic would quickly disappear.

Chapter Eleven

Who The Hell Are You?

On my first night I'd been strolling down Soi 7 and some woman grabbed my arm.

'I know you!'

I didn't recognise her from Adam. She told me that she'd been with me twice before and that I'd had a poorly eyeball. On my last holiday I had developed a terrible eye infection so to me this was irrefutable proof that she was telling the truth. I apologised to her and just said I'm always drunk so I forget a lot of people. I said goodbye and with that I carried on walking down the street.

On my third night I was sat chatting to my favourite Thai woman (just a friend) and also a couple she knew. The woman was Thai and the man was Indian, he owned a business out there. When he told me they had a child I instantly had to ask him a question just out of pure curiosity.

'The Thai gene is much stronger than the Caucasian gene, so white men's kids out here always looks Thai. Which gene wins out of the Indian gene and the Thai gene?'

He took out his phone and showed me a photo of his son. He looked purely Indian. He then laughed and said,

'The Indian gene wins'

It was during this conversation that I suddenly had a flashback and it was of me bumming a bargirl. To be honest this is something I rarely do in Pattaya. With an English woman it's pretty much a given. I think it's something to do with an English woman's big hanging red piss flaps not being as inviting as a Thai girl's tidy vagina. Anyway, I'm having this flashback of me bumming this girl and then suddenly....*Sweet Jesus*! I remembered it was that woman who'd grabbed my arm on the first night! I finished my drink, said my goodbyes and went straight to her bar.

I think the reason I'd forgotten her was because back then she'd had longer hair and couldn't speak a word of English. It's generally conversation that I remember more than sex. When I got to her bar I explained that I remembered her and why I'd forgotten her. I took her straight to my room as I fancied an early one.

After bumming her again we were laid in bed together and she was playing with her phone. I noticed her screensaver was a photo of her with a white man. I asked if it was her boyfriend and obviously it was. He was some Yank only in his twenties, she was the same age as me, although admittedly looked like she was in her twenties. I asked about him and she told me how much money he was sending her a month. It was around the equivalent of £600! What a complete idiot! I asked her if he fucked her in the arse as well and she replied,

'No, he not know I do that'

It's strange how much this city changes you. I remember on my first holiday I'd been really attracted to a woman but I knew she had a Norwegian husband so I never barfined her out of good conscience. Those morals of mine had diminished during my second trip there. You very quickly learn to go with the flow.

Later on in the night I was laid there with this woman's tongue as far up my rectum as she could possibly get it. At that moment I almost felt sorry for that silly young man. After we'd finished invading each other's bumholes I went and sat on the balcony for a smoke. The cloud formation in the sky above me was absolutely amazing, it was like nothing I'd ever seen before. The clouds basically looked like a huge tunnel going upwards and in the opening at the top a full moon was on show. It was like an oil painting.

One day I'll forget all about that woman and her Yank boyfriend but I will never ever forget that sky. Because that's just the type of guy I am.

Chapter Twelve

Piss

Have you ever drank human piss? I have once accidently during a cruel prank played on me when I was 17. Thai apple juice tastes exactly the same. Avoid it!

Chapter Thirteen

Is It A Man Or Is It A Woman? I'm Not Quite Sure But It's Definitely Got A Cock

The first week seemed to go by in a blur. There was one night I was sitting in a ladyboy bar, obviously right at the back out of sight of the street. I had a group of ladyboy's surrounding me and I noticed one had a tattoo covering the full length of his forearm and it was a declaration of love for a man. I asked if it was his boyfriend and he said no, it was just some bloke who paid him 30,000 baht to get it done and then he'd never seen him again. Then this other ladyboy showed me his arm and it was the exact same tattoo but on the inside of his arm. So basically there's some knob travelling around paying ladyboy's, possibly women as well to get his name tattooed on their arms! I remember exactly what the tattoo said and the man's name but I refuse to print it in this book. The mind boggle's at just how fucked up and cruel some men are. The ego of this man and the power trip he must receive from these tattoos makes me feel personally sick to the stomach! Obviously he is an utter penis. I can only guess that he is completely devoid of any personality. Maybe one day he might realise that if he actually had a personality it would be a far better way for people to remember him.

I ended up barfining a ladyboy from this bar and I did my usual of telling him to meet me outside my hotel in five minutes time. I know this upsets them but I have my reputation to think of.

When we were in bed he started deep throating me (as pointed out in previous books, a fairly easy thing to do with me). He made a point of keeping his lips firmly pressed down against the base of my Johnson for a fair few seconds. The greediness of it shocked me! As I watched him doing it I realised that I had completely fallen in love! The language barrier, culture barrier and gender barrier meant nothing to me at all. The love making was outstanding. If you've never shagged a ladyboy but you want to try it then I'll give you a top tip, get them to lay flat on their front, this massively decreases the chance of any penis viewage.

It was during this sweet lovemaking that I encountered a phenomenon I'd only ever heard about but never experienced. It was actually my ex-wife who'd told me about it. She had a lot of gay friends and she used to tell me all the sordid things they'd get up to. Stories so disgusting they make my books seem like children's books. One of her best friends was the 'top boy' and his boyfriend the 'bottom boy'. The story my ex told me was that whilst being hammered up the bum this bottom boy would ejaculate without his penis being touched!

So I've got this ladyboy laid on his front and I'm giving him a right good bumming. Suddenly he screams out,

'I cum! I cum!'

I could see both of his goddamn hands clutching the end of the mattress right in front of me! The only penis my own hands ever touch is my own. A wave of confusion passed over me but then I remembered about this bizarre phenomenon. This ladyboy must've loved cumming even more than me because he got me to bum him another two times that night and it happened again both times.

I was so in love that I actually let this one sleep overnight in my bed. When I awoke in the morning (afternoon is morning to me out there) my heart was in a flutter and I had a smile on my face. I opened my eyes, turned to look at my new found love and then realised that I had naked man laid next to me! I couldn't get him out of my room fast enough! I can't believe I've made that same mistake twice! Shame on me!

A couple of nights later I was sitting with that bargirl who had the Yank boyfriend and it turned out one of her mates had spotted me meeting this ladyboy outside my hotel. I told her in the politest possible way that I'll fuck anything. By now she knew how I talk so I said to her,

'If a dog walked through this bar right now I'd probably fuck that as well'
I can't say this joke went down very well because not even the corners of her mouth twitched in the slightest of ways. She simply said,

'Up to you'

Bargirl gossip is nearly as bad as British contractor's gossip. A line I used on her is also one I use on men I work with,

'The only people who talk about me are boring cunts with nothing else to talk about'

Chapter Fourteen

She Came Bearing A Gift

Surely by now I was two weeks into my holiday? I'd blown a good chunk of my budget but that was always to be expected. After such a long spell away I knew I'd go a bit mental at the start. I took my phone out of the safe (I don't bother with mobiles much on holiday, they never leave my hotel room) and I was absolutely horrified to find out I'd only been there nine days! You would think this would be a good thing but this was the first moment when I knew I was going to run into financial difficulty. I'd seriously under budgeted the holiday and it was mainly due to the drop in value to the pound. It was on this very same day though that my finances were only going to get worse because when I'd turned on my phone I had an email from Ann. If you don't know who Ann is, then all you need to know is that she is the only bargirl who I have ever genuinely cared about. (Although this still wasn't enough to stop me from trampling all over her feelings) Our last contact had been during my fifth holiday in November 2014. She'd sent me an email which read,

'I fucking hate you! I never want to see you again!' Our 'relationship' had always been a rocky one.

Early on during this holiday I'd been sat near her old bar and it had got me thinking about her. I'd asked one of the bargirls if I could use her phone and I sent Ann an email to let her know I was back in Pattaya. I got a quick response saying she was having personal problems and couldn't meet me. I wished her well and then forgot all about it. The email I received from Ann on day nine read,

'I need help. Can you help me?'

My heart sank as soon as I read it. I knew there was only one type of help she could need from me. I gave her my hotel name and room number knowing that I was only inviting grief to myself.

When the knock on the door came the first thing I noticed was the rash covering her forehead. I'd always known about her allergy but this was the first time I'd seen it. After she gave me a brief smile she dropped her head so that her hair fell in front of her face. She walked past me into the room sheepishly and the second thing I noticed was that she'd put on a bit of weight. She was wearing a black dress with frills and she was holding her handbag with both hands in front of her stomach.

I offered her a seat but she chose to lay down on the bed sideways, she spread the frills of her dress out and kept her handbag in front of her stomach. I asked about her allergy, she told me it had been really bad for a while now and then she told me some sob story about some mental ex-boyfriend and a bad break up. I wasn't interested, I've learned from personal experience never to listen to a woman's version of events when it comes to break ups. I cut to the chase,

'How long have you been pregnant?'
The fact that she was laid there trying to hide it from me was an insult to my very limited intelligence.

'15 weeks'
'So how do you want me to help you?'
'I need 10,000 baht'
I asked her about certain monies I knew she received and she explained them away quite well. She assured me I'd get the money back within a week. Probably about 40% of me believed this which in hindsight was very naïve of me.

10,000 baht is something you'd give a mate back home without thinking twice, but this was a Thai bargirl and all I had was a quickly diminishing holiday fund. Regardless of this fact laid in front of me was clearly a desperate woman and it was a woman who I have always liked. I consider myself to be a fairly hard-hearted man who doesn't suffer fools gladly, but this wasn't a con. It was someone who needed help and I found I couldn't refuse. Having said that I gave her 8000 baht instead of the 10,000 she'd asked for. She took it and said she had to go straight to the bank to deposit it.

After one hour she was back in my room. Even that rash on her face didn't diminish her looks. She slept over that night and we didn't discuss any of her problems, we just had a laugh. I'd forgotten how funny she was. All of her boyfriends have been English so she's been completely anglicised. She swears, she knows lots of English slang and this is the reason she has always been my favourite.

I can remember standing up off the bed to go out for a smoke and I turned and looked down at her laid on my bed.

'How the fuck did I end up with a pregnant woman laid in my bed? This could only happen to one man in Pattaya'

Jabbing my fingers into my chest

'Fucking me!'

She laughed and replied,

'That's 'cos you lucky man'

You're probably wondering at this point if I had sex with a woman who was nearly four months pregnant with another man's baby? This is me we're talking about…I've done worse things in life.

Chapter Fifteen

A Very Unhappy Ending

When Ann left the next day I felt stressed out about my money. So to cheer myself up I decided to spend a little bit more of it and ordered a massage through reception. Every time I'd spoken to the receptionist I'd made a point of saying 'happy ending'. This time I didn't say those two magic words because I'd reached a point where I thought every member of staff in that hotel had realised that I'm a complete slag. If they hadn't then there was definitely something wrong with them all.

When the masseur turned up little alarm bells started to ring in my head. Firstly she was wearing a different uniform to all the rest who'd come before her and also she didn't automatically go straight to the curtains and half close them like the others had done.

I laid on the bed bollock naked on my front and my hopes were raised when she rubbed her greased up hand straight through my arse cheeks. At the halfway point I was laid on my back and as she massaged the inside of my thighs 'little Toby' got a bit excited and started to twitch a bit. To alleviate my earlier concerns I asked the lady if she gave a happy ending. It turns out I do feel shame after all because I can remember feeling quite embarrassed as I asked her this question, I think it was because she was an older lady. To make things even more embarrassing she either didn't understand the term or maybe it was my accent. To my own horror I found myself pointing at my tiddle and then I started to simulate masturbation using my right hand. Luckily this sign language is internationally recognised, unluckily however she replied,

'No, me only do massage'

It instantly killed off my best friend and I spent the rest of the massage feeling incredibly pissed off. I wasn't pissed off with masseur of course, I admired her dignity, it was with the receptionist I'd phoned. Had her brain fallen out when I'd rang her? Laying there being massaged, instead of being relaxed I found myself fantasising about wrapping the receptionists telephone cord around her chest and using it to strangle her tits! Obviously this was something I was never going to do, the more practical solution would be to keep making a point of saying 'happy ending' whenever I rang.

To give credit to the masseur it was a heck of a massage and far from being the worst that I've had. That accolade goes to the massage I'd had in Mexico when I'd been on my honeymoon with that wanker. I'd paid a lot of money for me and her to have an hour massage each. We'd walked onto a big posh wooden staging on the beach and we were greeted by a smiling woman and a smiling man. My ex instantly whispered into my ear,

'That man is *not* putting his hands on me'
Cue one of the most awkward experiences of my entire life. That was probably the moment I knew I'd leave her one day.

P.S

Do you realise that I've just told you a story where literally nothing happened?

P.P.S

I actually scribbled this chapter down whilst sitting on my hotel toilet having a poo. This is something I shan't be doing again as I found it to be somewhat distracting.

Chapter Sixteen

Is It Me Or Is It My Body?

When I had my first night off the booze I slept a full 15 hours. Rather than waking up feeling groggy I actually felt really refreshed. I went straight to run a bath and when I turned on the tap I was instantly sprayed on the back of the head by a jet of cold water from the shower. I can tell you that this gets quite annoying after the sixth or seventh time of it happening.

It's worth pointing out that I have an obsession with cleanliness when I'm in Pattaya. I have a bath on the morning, a bath before I go out at night and also numerous showers. I remember before my first holiday I'd done some Pattaya research and I'd read that Thai's don't like the smell of white skin, it must be something to do with our different diets. A similar way to how we think Paki's stink. I must say though that I've never ever received any complaints about my smell out there, only compliments. (Apart from my first holiday, a couple of moans about my bellend but this problem was quickly remedied. Please refer to chapter 25 of Rigs, Pigs & Dirty Digs).

I realised that I had changed from this holiday to the previous ones during that first month. I didn't mix a single drink, I hadn't even touched a drop of lager. I didn't drink during the day at all, I always started at around 16:00. I was drinking less on the night time and I was always in my room before daylight. (When I say drinking less, I still completed my daily ritual of drinking a 35cl bottle of Sangsom on the balcony before going out) At the time I remember wondering if it was me getting older or if I just had a different mentality because it was such a long holiday? I did actually start to worry that maybe it was something to do with aging (I can actually give you the answer right now, it was definitely my mentality because everything you have just read went out of the window as the holiday progressed)

One thing that definitely hadn't changed about me was my distaste of the Indians who seemed to swamp my hotel! Savages that they are! Every one of them shared rooms with only one bed in. You can only imagine what the poor bargirls have to go through. They think they can just gangbang the girls like they would with their own daughters back home! They're also very rude. They generally aren't rude to whites, it's the Thai's they seem to speak down to. I remember walking through reception one day and one of them was yelling at the receptionist at the top of his voice. I was proud to see her shouting straight back at him. God knows what he was complaining about, these people seem to complain about anything at all. It was probably something ridiculous like the position of the sun in the sky!

There was one afternoon where I had a little run in with one of them. I was sunbathing by the pool and to my right was another westerner sunbathing. Two grown Indian men came in giggling like children and jumped straight into the pool. They were splashing around like a pair of gaylord's. After a time I watched one of them do a bomb into the pool and soak the other westerner. It was clearly on purpose. The man sat up and looked at them but didn't say anything. Ten minutes later they did the exact same thing to him. This time when he sat up he shook his head at them when he looked at them but he didn't actually say anything. I'm going to make an assumption that this man was European. Luckily because of the position of my sunbed and the surrounding tables and sunbeds they didn't have any room to do any bombs near me. However they couldn't help themselves could they, one swam passed me and made a point of splashing me as he did. I instantly gave him a death stare and said,

'Mate, don't ever fucking do that to me again'
He apologised with his silly nodding head,
    'Sorry, sorry'
It pissed me off enough that I had to stop sunbathing and go to my room. This is grown men we're talking about here! I also refused to use that pool after seeing

a load of them swimming in there one day. I know this sounds like blatant bigotry and the truth is it is. I've had good chats with some Indians at bars and back in England also but I really can't stand these beasts using the same hotel as me. If the mingebag's actually paid for separate rooms where the poor bargirls would feel safe then maybe I'll change my opinion of them. Dirty cunts!

Chapter Seventeen

Drama! Drama! Drama!

Day 17 was a bit of a flipping strange day for me. For a man like me who strives to avoid drama I certainly seem to attract a lot of it. The precursor to this drama started 4 or 5 nights earlier. I'd been sat at a bar with a girl and we'd already had a couple of brief chats earlier in the trip. She told me she was 23 and had worked in Pattaya for one year. Her English was very limited and we could just about manage half a conversation. (I must point out that I always learn new Thai words with every holiday and by the end of this one I was quite proud with the amount I'd learned. A lot of the words I had to think about when using or listening to but some words became so common that they might as well have been English when I heard them. I'm definitely not one of those ignorant Brit's)

She was younger than what I normally go for but I was thinking with my dick that night so I barfined her. A couple of nights later I went back to her bar but she was already sitting with some other bloke. I didn't say hello to her because I believe that's disrespectful to the man. I was looking everywhere except her direction but then she started cavorting with this man in such an extravagant way that it became hard to miss. I had a good idea of why she was doing it.

When it came to day 17 it started with me checking my messages and I'd received one from Ann ranting and raving at me. She had slept over a couple of nights previously, I'd told her I'd knock a 1000 baht off her debt every time she slept. That night I'd fed her and the next day I gave her enough for taxi fare. This raving message was about how I made her feel cheap! The audacity of the woman! I'm not a stupid man and I knew the real reason for this message. Actually there were two reasons for it. When she'd slept she had asked me to take her out but I point blank refused because I didn't want anyone thinking it was me who'd gotten her pregnant. This upset her but that wasn't my problem. The other reason for the message was so she could obviously start to get out of paying me my money back.

This message really pissed me off but I decided not to reply, regardless of everything she was having a tough time. I went out that night but I never quite shook off the mood that message put me in. I went back to that young girls bar and when I sat down she approached me,

'You don't like me!'

I asked her what she was talking about.

'I see you on balcony. Many women! I see you and I cry'

I was a bit taken aback by the last comment. I told her that she needed to toughen up and reminded her that she worked in Pattaya.

'You don't like me!'

With that she stormed off. I wasn't in the mood for this so I decided to go for a walk as I'd barely used my legs since I got there. I walked up to Soi 6 and was pleasantly surprised to find it heaving. On my last holiday it had been really quiet and I'd feared that infamous street might have been on the decline. I drank at a couple of bars but very quickly realised this was going to be one of my indecisive nights. (A night where it seems impossible to choose a woman). From Soi 6 I walked to Soi Buakhao, a place I've never liked for some reason. I didn't even stop at a bar. From there I made my way to Walking Street. By now I was completely sick of walking and I needed a poo so I jumped on a baht bus back to Soi 7 and relieved myself in the hotel. (On the toilet of course, not in the middle of reception)

I decided I wanted to get my hand back into playing pool so I jumped from bar to bar on Soi 7 playing pool with different women. Eventually I found myself playing pool with an attractive woman who had an athletic body. I asked if she would like to come out for a drink with me and she told me she had school the next day! I was very perplexed as she was clearly above school age. She explained she was a 25 year old mature student and she studied two days a week. Then she showed me some bizarre photos of her at school wearing a uniform! (I'm going to start saying college because 'school' just sounds wrong) I should've been impressed with her ambition but inside all I felt was disappointment. I'd finally found a girl I wanted to barfine and I wasn't even able to. She asked if I could meet her the next night because she'd be able to have a drink. I left the bar and thought,

Fuck it I'll just have a drink on my own on the balcony

I was about to walk into a shop near my hotel when I heard my name being called out. As I was turning around to see who it was a pair of drunken arms wrapped themselves around my waist

'You don't like me!'

It was that young lass. I told her to sit on a bench nearby, I went in the shop and bought myself some whisky and her a litre of water.

'Why don't you like me?'

'I do like you, why do you think I don't like you?'

'You have many women'

'I'm a butterfly, I told you I was a butterfly when I barfined you'

'I want be with you tonight'

I took her back to my room and when she sat on my bed she actually started crying!

'I feel different for you'

'Don't feel different for me, I'm the same as everyone else. Same as that man you were with the other day'

'No, no, he just customer'

'I'm just a customer. Same, same. I don't want you to like me'

'I know, not understand, just feel different for you. I see you everyday'

With that she laid down on the bed and started crying again. If you've never been to Pattaya then the thought of an attractive young woman crying over you probably sounds brilliant. Trust me it isn't, I felt terrible.

After she'd calmed down it turned out that she'd told me some fibs. She wasn't 23 she was 21 and she hadn't been in Pattaya a year it had only been 5 months. When girls lie about these two things it's usually the other way around.

I knew that whatever this girl thought she felt for me was born purely out of confusion and not having adjusted to the Pattaya head fuck yet. I felt genuinely sorry for her. The next day when she was sober I tried my best to give her some advice and I also told her to never put me in that situation again. I never barfined her for the rest of the holiday. It didn't take long for her to stare at me with daggers in her eyes when I walked past. Hatred is a far easier emotion for me to deal with.

Chapter Eighteen

This Has Never Happened To Me Before

On day 19 I didn't get out of bed until 17:00. I'd spent the day sleeping and having sex with that student. I had actually toyed with the idea of keeping her for a few days but she had a really busy lifestyle and it meant most days of the week she was up early. I couldn't allow the risk of someone waking me up early everyday so unfortunately I had to let her go, which was a bit of a shame.

Later on in the night I was sitting with a bargirl I'd known for years, her English is impeccable. During this conversation I had another one of my 'profound' drunken insights and unfortunately for you I'm going to tell you it. (This is my book after all so I should get some sort of say of what goes in it)

We were chatting away and at one point she told me that she felt like she had two different people living inside of her. I told her that I was the same. I then discreetly pointed at a man across the bar and said he'll be the same and then I pointed at a bargirl and said she'd be the same. I explained that everyone has certain thoughts and they wonder to themselves if other people think the same things as them. I told her we're all the same and this is the point when I came out with my line of the day,

'Only when you realise that all people are the same does that make you different'

In hindsight rather than garbling all of that nonsense I probably should've just told her she had ADD.

Later on I was in one of my favourite haunts watching a band when a good looking western couple came and sat next to me. I heard their foreign accents and assumed they were Russian. In my opinion this planet is far too small a place for Russians to exist. By this point I was quite inebriated and carefree,

'Ere mate, are you a Russian?'

He turned and looked at me, he smiled a smile that lit up his face, offered me his hand and informed me that he was Dutch. That charming smile and gentlemanly handshake instantly won me over. We began chatting and I told him my stories about working in the Netherlands in my younger days. He was intelligent, humorous and the conversation flowed. I was introduced to his wife who came and stood directly in front of my face. She had a set of sparkling blue eyes that were easy to get lost in. She told me she could speak seven different languages, a sure sign of high intelligence. I asked her my favourite question that I ask every multi-linguist that I meet,

'What language do you think in?'

'It depends on which country I'm in'

Before too long she went off to speak to a bargirl that they both liked the look of. Me and him were staring at the pair of them chatting away. He was telling me how much he loved her. He then flippantly asked me if I'd like to come with the three of them and that we could 'swap'. He was being deadly serious but I laughed out loud and said,

'You are *so* fucking European'

I went onto explain that banging another man's wife in front of him had no appeal to me. The truth is I would've loved to have shagged his wife but I didn't want him seeing my little tiddle, I'd been left with absolutely no doubt that he had a rather generous one.

It was a pleasure to spend time with that couple, moments like that are what holidays are all about. When they left I was eyeing up a beautiful looking girl who was sitting a few bars away. We'd been giving each other glances before that Dutch couple had arrived. I started heading to her bar but before I'd even got there she was waving her hand at me and beckoning me over. I must have sat with her for at least one hour before we left that bar together.

As soon as we were walking down the street away from the noise of the band I noticed a deepness to her voice that I hadn't picked up on earlier. Alarm bells rang and I looked for all the signs. She had a slightly high forehead but this along with pouting lips is what gave her an exotic look. I looked at her throat, there wasn't a hint of an Adams apple. Her hands and feet weren't small but they couldn't be classed as large either. She asked if we could play pool so I took her to the quietest bar I could see whilst I tried to figure out exactly what she was. The drunker she got her voice became a little deeper and when I noticed how incredibly skinny her legs were I was now 90% sure it was a ladyboy. 10% of me clung onto the hope that I might be wrong.

By the time we got to my room I knew I'd been conned. I didn't even ask, I just grabbed the crotch and sure enough it definitely wasn't a vagina in my hand. It's with some shame that I must admit that I hit the roof. I said something's I shouldn't have said. You might be wondering at this point what my problem was? Surely a man who doesn't mind banging the odd bloke would be happy that he'd discovered the most realistic, beautiful ladyboy he'd yet been with? I shall tell you for why. Banging ladyboy's is something I do discreetly through the backdoor…if you'll pardon the pun. I'd been sat at a busy bar with this ladyboy for over an hour, surrounded by other bars, some of which I knew the girls in. I had then walked through the streets side by side with him to another bar. Also my pride had been dented. Back home many men have told me stories about their mates who've been 'caught out'. I've always said to them,

'Your mate is full of shit, you can always tell'

Although technically I wasn't caught out I know some other men would've been. I hereby apologise to anyone whose story I have ever doubted.

It didn't take me long to calm down and have him literally bollock naked. Many men have asked me if it's true that ladyboy's are better looking than women. Overall no but in some cases definitely yes, one thing they do have is better bodies. This one was on all fours on my bed with a tiny little arse and ribcage showing. The sight of his waxed little bullethole winking would tempt most men to put their penis in there.

When I woke up the next day I went to have a poo and the dirty bastard had left a little bit of shit on the toilet seat! I was forced into wiping it off with tissue. After a while you get used to seeing other people's faecal matter and also blood. Pattaya can be a messy business.

That night perfectly sums up Pattaya for me. If you put the effort in you can have interesting conversations with bargirls, you can meet interesting people from all over the world and during every second of the day there's perversions going on. Whether its gangbangs, swinging, men having sex with men who look like women, men having sex with men who look like men and everything in between.

Chapter Nineteen

Christmases Without Presents Are Always The Best

On Christmas Eve me and a bargirl double-teamed a pair of young Danish men. I'm happy to report that we won all three games of pool. One of the Danish men was enjoying his first ever trip to Pattaya, I told him I bet he was having the best time of his entire life. He agreed that he was. The other Danish man was on his second holiday there. I said to him,

'Is it different this time for you mate? Not as good?'

The reply was what I expected, he wasn't having as good a time as his first. I tried to console him.

'The first time you come all you see are the neon lights. The second time you see past the lights and realise that this isn't a very nice place. Don't worry mate, your third holiday you'll love it again. You just learn to go with the flow'

I woke up in a hotel room on Christmas day for the second time in my life. Luckily this time it was in Pattaya instead of Aberdeen. This was my first ever Christmas abroad and at no point in the day did it feel like Christmas at all. Even when I went for Christmas dinner in The Pig & Whistle Pub did it feel Christmassy. Yet again this was another Christmas Day when some stranger decided to read about my life, I don't know whether to feel pity or privilege?

I'd started the day by emailing Ann and telling her she could keep the money she owed me as Christmas present. This was one of those selfish gifts where it's really for yourself. I knew there was no chance of me getting that money back but that message made me feel good about myself. I have absolutely no regrets about helping Ann out but I'll never do it again. Not with any bargirl.

On the night I was doing my usual of playing pool with a girl and there was a couple waiting in the wings. When we finished the man asked if he could play me as apparently the woman he was with wasn't very good. He was in his late fifties and he had a broad Scouse accent. When he told me that he'd lived in Australia since he was eleven years old I had nothing but respect for the man. I've always believed that people who lose their accents are completely fake and aren't to be trusted. His name was Glen and the more I talked to him the more I liked him. He had one of those personalities where you could sit and listen to him all day long...I barely let him get a word in! I asked him if the woman he was with was his girlfriend,

'Sort of. She's my Pattaya girlfriend.'

This common sense approach made me respect him even more. He went on to tell me how they had first met. Five years earlier he'd been sat at a bar and he'd told the Mamasan that he wanted four girls to take back to his room. He said he wanted good girls who didn't mind getting their hands dirty. When he was having this one man orgy one girl in particular had stood out from the rest by the sheer amount of effort she was putting in. In the end he'd chased the other three out of the room and kept this one good one. There they were five years later still together.

It was such a heartfelt and moving love story that I almost had to catch a tear when he finished telling me it. Again this was another person who it was a pleasure to meet.

Later on that night I wanted to give myself a Christmas present. I'd never ever had a soapy massage in all my time spent in Pattaya so I thought this might be the perfect treat. A taxi bike took me to a hotel sized building just off Second Road. I was led inside by a Thai man and I was struck at just how posh this place was. After walking down a corridor it opened up into a large room resembling something from ancient Rome. There were large pillars from floor to ceiling and either side of me were staggered seats full of women. Each lady had a coloured badge with a number on it.

My male guide informed that the blue badges were 2500 baht and the green badges were 3000 baht. He didn't even show me the girls on the other side of the room so I'm assuming he thought I was cheap scum. He was correct, I only had 3000 baht on me so I picked a blue badge girl. I made the mistake of picking the best looking of a bad bunch, I'm fairly sure the uglier ones probably put more effort in. Once I picked the girl she led me to a lift and took me up to the second floor. The room we ended up in was huge, posh and far better than my hotel room. On the left was a hot tub sized bath and on the floor next to it an inflatable mattress. The bed was queen size and God knows what inch the telly was but it was huge and playing a music channel.

As she filled the bath I was told to strip naked. Once in it she washed every inch of me (apart from my hair which I told her not to touch). After the bath I laid on the mattress in a very gingerly fashion, the wet tiled floor was a death trap! Once laid down she covered me in soap suds and proceeded to massage me using her entire body. The feeling of having your ballsack massaged by a pair of wet tits is quite wonderful.

When it came to sex I was surprised to see her putting a condom on me before oral! I can only assume that the usual clientele are Arab and this is good practice with those filthy savages. When I mounted her there was a certain coldness to the sex that I wasn't used to, it was pretty obvious she didn't want to be there. I actually went limp. She asked me what was wrong,

'I don't know, I've never done this before. It's different than being with a girl from a bar'

After I said that she laid me on my back, whipped of the condom and started piping me off properly. She was really going for it. After a time she was sat on my face. The soapy scent of her clean shaven vagina was lovely. (If the thought of sticking your tongue in a hole that's had a thousand cocks in it turns your stomach then I deeply apologise) After a lifetime of studying porn I'd like to believe that I'm quite proficient at oral sex. She had an ultra-sensitive clit and her grunting blowjob quickly turned into a moaning clumsy wank. After a while she was just grabbing onto my ankles and wriggling about. I was back in the mood for it after that.

The verdict? 5 stars for the massage and 3 stars for the sex. Was it worth £50? Not really but I'm glad I did it. When I left I was still amazed that such a huge posh building existed purely for sex. I've heard all sorts of stories about Pattaya that I've still yet to witness, huge swimming pool orgies and the like. What a truly remarkable place it is.

The next day I rang my parents for the first time to ask how Christmas had went. I was talking to my dad and he asked if I'd had a good day.

'Yeah it was good, I went and had a soapy massage'

He then said,

'Our Chris has bought me and your mam one of those for Christmas'

I started laughing out loud. He corrected himself

'Well, probably not the same as what you had'

'I can guarantee it won't be the same'

Bless the silly old fool.

Part Three

I Think I Quite Like It Here

Chapter Twenty

New Year's Grieve

For many years now I've been puzzled as to why we changed our New Year from the start of spring (in the good old Middle Ages) to the middle of winter. I know it's based on the Winter Solstice, but surely a new year starts in the 'season of life' rather than in the middle of the 'dead season'? The view from my balcony finally helped me to understand the change. I'd been able to enjoy the sunsets on most evenings and when I first arrived the sun was setting behind the high rise buildings on the Pattaya south coast. It was actually setting directly behind the middle building and when the sun was halfway behind the top of the building it created the largest phallic symbol that I have ever seen. The sun would look like an enormous glowing bellend. Day by day I watched the sun move slowly to the left and then it finally reached a point where it couldn't go any further and started heading back to the right. Only in a sunny climate do you appreciate what the Solstice is all about. By the time I left Pattaya the sun was setting behind the island of Koh Lan.

It was on my balcony that I spent New Year's Eve, completely sober and alone. The vantage point was perfect for the firework displays in the north, south and everywhere in between. I was sober for a couple of reasons. One, my stomach was in pieces and my farts had actually started to smell like Pattaya itself. Two, I hate New Year, I always have. The Millennium is the only one I can ever remember enjoying. There was something special about the turn of a century, plus I was off my tits on Ecstasy.

The main reason I hate New Year is because I really, really can't stand being told what to do. I'm not going to be told I have to go out just because it's a certain number of a month.

'But you're *supposed* to go out'

Fuck that! It's the same reason I don't celebrate my birthday. Why celebrate getting older? Maybe I'm just a miserable twat or maybe everyone else is wrong?

New Year's Day is always a sombre affair in the West and I was surprised to find that even in Pattaya I felt sombreness. It was only for one reason though, I could no longer say,

'I'm not going back home until next year'

I was sitting on my balcony soaking up the rays feeling quite miserable when I suddenly remembered a text message I'd received the day before. It was from a friend congratulating me on achieving everything I said I was going to do in 2017. That one thought completely changed my mood and I sat there feeling quite proud of myself. To celebrate I cracked open a bottle of whisky and toasted myself. It was only early but in the spirit of the moment I decided to finish off the bottle. By the end of that night I was as drunk as a butcher's cat.

It turned out that there were some kid's bellies out that night who were even more pissed than me. I'd walked down Soi 8 and a man walked past with blood streaming from both of his nostrils. Further up the street an angry looking man with a torn shirt was being calmed down by a group of mates. This moment incredibly disappointed me, it was the first genuine trouble I'd seen between tourists. Luckily I didn't see anything similar for the remainder of the holiday. Nearly ten months of my life spent in that city and all I've seen is some Thai girls fighting, a man with a bloody nose and a handful of arguments. I can still say comfortably that I feel a lot safer on a night out in Pattaya than I do on a night out in any British town.

That drunken fool celebrated the start of the year with a completely broken nose. I'll leave it up to you to guess what nationality they were.

Chapter Twenty-One

Born On The Fourth Of January

The 4th January 2018 was quite a special day for me, five years previously I had taken my first footsteps in Pattaya on this very day. It had been the start of a brand new life for me. However my fifth year anniversary wasn't as good as what it should've been.

The night before I'd barfined a girl, she was about 5' tall, stick thin, covered in tattoos and had short hair. You know the type, they're normally seen with meatheads. I'd enjoyed her company so I'd invited her out with me the next night. This was the first time this holiday that I'd actually taken a woman out with me at the start of the night. I regretted it almost instantly. For a slag like me it's no fun having to spend all night drinking with one woman. A couple of times I thought about telling her to go back to her bar but she seemed to be enjoying herself, I knew I'd feel guilty afterwards if I'd done that. I'd promised her a night out so I suppose I had to stick to it. This is the reason why, the older I get, the less promises I make to people because they always end up setting me back.

Late on in the night we were both a touch drunk and she went in a mood with me for some reason or other. I'll never understand the bargirl mentality, from a business point of view it leaves little to be desired. In Pattaya women with normal jobs are also readily available but this is something I've always avoided out of fear of how they'd react the next day when I ask them to leave. With a money binding contract there's no such worries, or should I say there aren't supposed to be any worries. With some of the girls if you barfine them more than once they behave as if they own you! Her mood would've been the ideal opportunity to get rid of her but now I was drunk and I was looking at her little frame, I decided better of it.

As we were sitting there I started pondering on the last five years of my life. My Pattaya life had started in the late stages of the age of 31 and now I was sat there in the late stages of 36. I'd packed so much into that time that it really did feel like five years. It actually should've felt even longer. I also had a little flashback to a job I'd been on the previous August. The rig itself had been a good laugh but the job was very grim. It was confined space work, I was working in a big metal box made from 40 year old rusted steel. Without the dim lighting it would've been pitch black. It was very much like being in a dungeon, something you'd see in a horror film. I was sitting having a breather with my colleague and we were chatting away.

'This is the type of shit I have to do to have my holiday's brother.'

'Aye you'll remember this when you're out there and it'll all seem worthwhile.'

That lovely little man had been very correct in his statement.

When I got Mrs. Grumpy back to my room she asked if she could wear one of my T-shirts. I'm a man who stands at 5'11", I have a 33" waist and a 42" chest. The only people who could ever describe me as big are midgets and men with no legs. When she put it on it looked like a nightie on her! It was akin to me wearing one of John Candy's T-shirts. That's how small she was!

I only saw this woman one more time. I was in my room one night and she'd texted me asking if she could come over. When she turned up at my door I was pleasantly surprised to see she had another girl with her. They both walked in the room and I introduced myself to her friend. I felt confused when this tag-along told me she was going back to the bar. When she walked out I asked,

'Did you just want her to meet me or something?'

'Crazy man at bar. He keep looking at me and following me'

Apparently this strange individual was only in his twenties. You wonder what goes through some men's minds when they're in a city full of prostitutes yet they want to harass one who has absolutely no interest in them.

On the subject of strange people I learned that a bargirl had been killed during this holiday. The story told to me was that an English squaddie threw a girl from his balcony. He claims that she fell. The weird thing is I didn't hear this story from a Thai source, it was a mate back in England who'd texted me about it. When I brought this story up with a couple of the bargirls they were quite blasé about it all.

It makes you really appreciate what these women have to go through each night. They never really know the man they're walking down the street with until they're back in his room.

Chapter Twenty-Two

True Love...Pattaya Style

You may recall me having a conversation with a woman who possibly suffered from ADD? I've known her now for four years. She has a very exotic face which stems from her father being a foreigner. She's very thin, a body to die for. Although she's four years older than me she looks younger than me (those lucky blummin Thai genes!). The poor woman is incapable of having children but it means she's maintained a washboard stomach which is hard to the touch. Washboard stomachs are a personal fetish of mine, easy to find in a gogo bar but surprisingly difficult to find in the normal bars. This lady is intelligent, she can speak three languages, of which English is her third and she spent 12 years of her life living in Europe. Her two favourite types of music are jazz and opera. As you can tell from this description she isn't your typical bargirl. I have never once barfined this woman. I can hear you shouting,

'Why in God's name not?!'

I'd like to take this opportunity to answer that question. The very first time I'd walked in her bar I'd immediately been accosted by an attractive woman who I'd ended up barfining. If I'd seen her first I would've chosen her over this other woman.

I think this is a good opportunity to clear something up. I'm a deeply shallow man and I always have been. (Shallow men always end up getting divorced) Naturally I've shagged my fair share of pigs in life but one man's pig is another man's princess. You see many men in Pattaya go for the 'girlfriend experience'. Sometimes I look at these men and I think to myself

Why have you chosen her?
I know a dog is man's best friend but surely there are limitations? Maybe these men are insecure or maybe they're just far nicer people than what I am?

So as I was saying I barfined the wrong girl that night and the girl I did choose turned out to be a bit psychotic. There was no way I'd break the 'one bar one girl' rule with her and risk causing a scene. Luckily one time when I went back to that bar the psycho was sat with another man so I was able to go and sit and have a conversation with this exotic looking woman. This was when I found out how good her English was. Over time it just became normal for me to go and sit and chat with her.

When you're a man who holidays alone and prefers talking to Thai's rather than other tourists then finding women with a good grasp of English is really important. When you do find them you shouldn't do anything to jeopardise that friendship. Hence the reason I've never barfined her but admittedly I've always had an urge to.

I mentioned that on Christmas Day I'd been playing pool with a girl before meeting Glen. This was the woman I was playing with, it had been our first game of pool together and we were flirting with each other quite outrageously. Without a bar in between us a lot of bodily contact was being made. At the time I remember thinking that maybe finally barfining her would be my ideal Christmas present. When Glen came along she must have felt a bit side-lined because after a time she went and sat behind the bar. When I finished playing pool with him I went to go and speak to her but she turned her back on me and refused to talk to me. I now understood what she meant when she told me she was two different people. I really don't have time for petty behaviour like this. We didn't speak for the next two weeks.

One night I was very drunk and decided to end this silly stalemate between us. She seemed happy to see me and told me she'd been upset that I'd ignored her when playing pool with Glen. Before I went in that bar I already knew I was going to barfine her. If I'm going to have fallouts with women then I might as well at least be having sex with them. When I asked her she said yes immediately.

Before going to my room we popped into a shop and I was surprised when she asked me to buy her Smirnoff Ice, I'd never seen her drink alcohol in all the years that I'd known her. When we sat on the balcony I asked her why she was drinking,

'I've waited four years for this moment. I need to feel calm'

Obviously when a beautiful woman says something like that to you then you're going to feel a bit happy about it. But that comment gave me a tinge of nervousness also. When you've known an attractive woman for a number of years, be it a friend, a work colleague or even a hooker then when this moment finally arrives nervousness is a natural emotion for anyone. You basically have an obligation to make them cum. To overcome this sensation I asked her if she wanted to go to bed. It seemed pointless sitting there and letting a feeling like that build up.

It turned out this lovely, sensible little woman was an absolute sexual predator! It's always the quiet ones! Some women were born to have sex and she was one of them. At one point she dragged me off the bed and 'made' me bang her against the wall. The hair pulling was my idea but the spanking was something she asked me to do to her. She had a big biff and I had a hard time filling it but luckily she was ultra-sensitive. She wasn't a squirter but she was a messy cummer, there was definitely no faking it with this one. We did some pretty disgusting things to each other.

The next day I felt bruised, battered and emotionally exhausted. I now consider myself to be a victim of rape. (I don't know why these female victims moan so much, I quickly got over the trauma of it)

After that first night I gave her the nickname 'Tiger'. In turn she nicknamed me 'Murderer'. This is nothing I haven't heard before. I have a fixed furrowed brow which gives me quite a serious look. You would think that looking like a killer would mean people would leave you alone but unfortunately for me I've found the opposite to be true.

I was to spend the next four days with her and they were some of the best days of the holiday so far, a chance to relax properly. Any man in the world would've felt lucky being with her. Intelligent, interesting and absolute filth. There are two types of bargirl in Pattaya, those who walk around the room wrapped in a towel and those who walk around completely naked. The latter are the best and Tiger had no qualms about walking onto my balcony in broad daylight completely naked.

I remember one day she was telling me how hard it had been to adjust back to Thai culture after living in Europe for so long. She was talking about how efficient and organised Europeans are and she was frustrated that Thai's couldn't be the same. I told her the answer was education. If you give a child a good education when they become adults they want to make their surroundings a better place. It used to be the same in England but those days are gone. Our education system these days is just a breeding ground for ultra-left-wing fascists who have absolutely no concept of people or reality. Their mission in life seems to be to destroy their own country rather than making it better.

Tragedy follows me everywhere and unfortunately my time with Tiger ended tragically. I was at a bar with her and that dark side of her personality came out, she behaved in a very idiotic manner. The two emotions I utilise in life the most are feeling happy and feeling pissed off, the switch between them can be flipped in a nanosecond. I quietly finished my drink, paid the bill and set off to my room without saying a word to her. She followed behind around ten feet back. When we were in the lift I didn't say a word and I could feel her staring at me. When we got to the room I asked her, calmly, to get her stuff and go back to her bar. She was graceful enough not to cause a scene. As she left I offered her 1000 baht but she told me ram it. This cheered me up only very slightly. Why can't things ever be simple?

Chapter Twenty-Three

A Truly Horrific Experience

One day my mobile decided that it wanted to stop working. With a heavy heart I set off to remedy the problem. The minute I stepped out onto the street I realised that my brain was very much like my phone...completely broken. Walking with a fragile head my leg/arm co-ordination seemed very rusty and I had to concentrate on every step. I stared at the floor the entire time as any human contact would've destroyed me at that point. It was a very cloudy day so I couldn't even wear sunglasses to use as a comfort blanket! (People who wear sunglasses on unsunny days are cunts! (Is "unsunny" a word? Yes it is, I've just googled it) Those wankers who sunglasses on the back of their heads are even bigger cunts!) Walking past the busy bars on Beach Road was particularly horrible. For the entire length of those bars I felt like I had eyes on me.

I was heading to a building that I've never stepped foot in before, The Central Festival Shopping Centre. It's a building I've always avoided and I would've died a happier man keeping it that way. When I walked in it was even worse than what I ever could've imagined it to be...completely rammed with human beings! How I managed to walk through it without having a complete nervous breakdown is a miracle.

I went in three different phone shops, each time having the same frustrating conversation.

'I need a phone for my English sim card please'

'You want Thai sim card?'

'No I want a phone'

'OK you choose'

'Yes but it has to fit my sim card'

'You want Thai sim card?'

'No I want a phone'

'OK, you choose'

I could go on but I'd end up annoying myself. It turns out my sim card is a bit outdated and these new stupid ones are a lot smaller. When I finally found the right phone it was two hundred bastard quid! (Thinking back, I was probably being taken advantage of there) I just wanted to get the fudge out of there so I grudgingly handed the lady my bank card and put my pin number into the machine.

'This card not work sir'

At this point I had to stop myself from swearing. I told them wankers at the bank that I was going to Thailand and would be using my card! When she handed me the card back she told me to phone the number in the corner of the card. I bit my tongue! The reason I was standing there in the first place must've completely gone over her head. When I walked back to hotel it was more of a march and I didn't care about

all the silly people I had to walk past, I was far too
pissed off to notice them.

Chapter Twenty-Four

Dear Oh Dear

I was incredibly happy that my bank card hadn't worked. It gave me time to remember that all my phone numbers are synced to my email account. I spent £40 on a smart phone with a Thai sim card. The first person I texted was Tiger. It had been five nights since my little spat with her and I decided it was time to bury the hatchet. When I sat down in her bar she didn't look very pleased to me but she came and sat with me regardless. Due to the look she was giving me I asked her if she was angry with me.

'You're stone'

'What?'

'You're made of stone. I'm a strong lady but I'm human'

'I'm human too, I wouldn't be sat here now if I wasn't. Look I'm not sorry for what I did but I'm sorry for the way I did it.'

That was the best sort of apology I could muster to take the tension away, truth be told I wasn't sorry about anything at all, she had behaved like a complete idiot. Unfortunately women are a different species to us men and they need to hear things like this. What we did both agree on though was that ignoring each other was completely childish. After this the conversation became normal and I tried my best to coax a smile out of her.

Inevitably we ended up in my bed having sex. After a while the sex started to become rough and then it got rougher and rougher. I've had some pretty rough sex with filthy English women but nothing on this scale. It reached a level that can only be described as sadism. At one point I abruptly stopped and said,

'I can't do this'

With that I went and sat outside for a smoke.

'What's wrong darling?'

'That's not normal'

I'm chuckling as I'm writing this, I don't consider myself to be a drama queen but that's exactly what I was at this point in time. I was sitting there looking out to sea and she was stood behind me with her arms wrapped around me. It was as if we'd had a gender role reversal with her trying to console me.

'It's inside of you, you have to let it out'

'I don't think I want to'

'There is only you and me, no one can see us'

When we went back to bed the sex was very normal and I was glad for it. Probably boring for her though. The next day we were laid there discussing this little escapade and I asked her if she'd learned all that stuff in Europe. She laughed and said 'No', she told me European men had always been scared of her and thought she was a psycho. I could see their point. She explained to me that's just how she is. At one point she asked me,

'Have you ever played with candles?'

'No I haven't. I'll try it if you want but you won't be doing it to me though'

The night before she'd asked if she could watch me whilst I had a piss, this gave me the confidence to say,

'I've never pissed on a woman, I wouldn't mind trying that'

She giggled and said,

'No problem'

'I'll have to be drunk to do all that stuff though'

Typically English of me, Dutch Courage. (I realise that line won't make any sense to people outside of the UK. Just google Dutch Courage)

She left to go home and pick up some clothes and I remember thinking,

She's beautiful, her body is perfect, she's clever and she is absolutely filthy. Right now I must be the luckiest man in Pattaya.

To give you an idea of how attractive she is there was one time we were in a lift together and a creepy Cockney bloke who was in there with us whispered into my ear,

"Nice"

I'm assuming he was talking about her and not paying me a compliment.

It turned out that we didn't do either of those perverse things, I think she was expecting me to go out and buy candles, which was never going to happen. A few nights later we did have a memorable encounter though. It started, quite bizarrely, with a song. Tiger had told me she loved opera, the only thing resembling opera on my IPod is Barcelona by Queen. There are some songs that give you a little shiver when you hear them however with her when she liked a song the shiver was more of a sexual reaction. (Like I said earlier some women are just born for sex)

I remember asking her if she had ever listened to Pink Floyd and she hadn't. She'd drank a bottle of Smirnoff, which was more than enough to get her drunk and I decided to play her The Great Gig In The Sky. I've never seen anyone react to music in such a way, she practically had an orgasm!

'This song makes me horny'

'It's from an album called Dark Side Of The Moon. It's voted the number one album in the world to have sex to'

With that she took off her thong and placed her feet up on the balcony guardrail with her legs wide open. I took the opportunity to rub her clit and finger her fufu. After a time I stood up in front of her, lowered my shorts and placed my penis in her mouth. Not wanting my testicles to feel left out I withdrew and then placed them on her tongue. I lifted her out of the chair with the intention of going on the bed but instead she bent over and put her hands against the sliding doors. If anyone on Soi 7 with decent eyesight had looked up at that point (which some people possibly might have) they would've seen my white arse moving backwards and forwards and my right hand making a slapping motion. I'm not an exhibitionist so the novelty of it quickly wore off. I took her to bed and put on Dark Side Of The Moon. That turned out to be the best sex I've ever had in Pattaya. I'll never listen to that album the same again.

I really liked Tiger but I only had one bugbear with her. Because she held herself like a true lady I had to be careful of my choice of words around her. I'd picked up some of the Thai English slang, such as saying 'same same'. If I used this slang with her she would roll her eyes at me and tell me to stop it. For her it was an insult to her intelligence. Also I had to curb my profanity a touch. Obviously I still swore, it's an impossibility for me not to swear but things such as the 'C word' would be frowned upon. When I say 'C word' I mean 'cunt'.

I spent seven days with Tiger which puts her on a par with Ann for the longest single stint I've had with a bargirl. No other bargirls have ever even come close to this. With me however, I always end up getting bored, no matter how good they are. I told her I'd like a few days on my own and there was no drama at all. I wished Ann could've behaved like this on my fourth holiday, it would've made it far more enjoyable. Both these women know my mind better than most, Tiger respected it but Ann would always try to change it. Tut, tut, tut.

Chapter Twenty-Five

Nightmares In A Damaged Brain

I'm hoping that at least one person who reads this book realises that chapter title is stolen from an obscure 1980's video nasty. Much like that film, this chapter is pretty shit.

One guarantee that I have on every trip to Thailand is that I will suffer from incredibly vivid dreams throughout the holiday. Some dreams are surreal, some are horrific but mainly they're about me having nights out in Pattaya. It's quite often that I'll wake up confused about what really happened the night before and what was in actual fact just a dream. It normally takes my sozzled brain a couple of minutes to figure out which was which. For instance one morning I woke up believing I'd had a huge argument with some bloke which had bordered on becoming a fight only to realise after a time it had only been a dream. I'm left in no doubt that these dreams are caused by nothing else but alcohol.

If I have nightmares out there they can be quite horrific, one terrible dream this holiday woke me up with such a start that I couldn't get back to sleep after waking from it. (I'm still praying for the day where I have a dream about me raping the false prophet Muhammad)

One incredibly vivid dream was about my ex best mate dying and the guilt of not reconciling with him before he died. In this dream I'd been deeply upset. The next day that dream had had such an effect on me that I contemplated texting his brother to put into motion a reconciliation. As my head cleared though and my brain became more focussed I remembered exactly what that tit had done and then thought better of it.

I was trying my best to have one night off the booze per week (which I gave up on halfway through the holiday) but on these sober nights the dreams would actually be even worse! I can only assume that these were caused by alcohol withdrawal.

I'm going to tell you an anecdote now which at first may seem completely irrelevant to this chapter but don't worry all will be made clear in the end.

There's a famous story floating around the oil rigs in the North Sea about a certain tradesman who takes his family to Thailand. Many, many people have told me this story and at first I didn't believe it. After hearing it so many times though I started to believe that there may be some truth to it but in all probability the story was surely embellished. Eventually I ended up working on a rig that this man had actually worked on and the story was told to me by a man who'd been given a first-hand account. I was shocked to find out that every bit of the story is actually true.

This man takes his wife and kids to Thailand, I don't know how often, possibly annually. Each night he drugs all their drinks, it has never been made clear to me exactly what drug he uses, rohypnol has been mentioned but I can't confirm whether that's true or not. Once they're all soundly asleep he goes out and does what every man would do on his own on a night out in Thailand.

For me personally there's a few things I can't fathom. What sort of a functioning brain would allow a man to drug his own children? What sort of brain would allow a father to leave his kids with a drugged up woman in a foreign land? Most importantly of all, what sort of brain would allow a man to boast about doing such things to his workmates?! He is obviously a *very* fucked up individual. If he loves Thailand so much why doesn't he just get a divorce?

Every time I've heard this story it always ends with the same punchline, which is what ties it into this chapter. Apparently his wife is known to say to people,

'I love going to Thailand, I always seem to get the best night's sleep there'

Chapter Twenty-Six

The Depression Of A Very Silly Boy

January 16th, what a horrible day that was. When I'd written about my first and second holidays I had described days of feeling depressed. I wised up to the fact that the main cause was the different amount of drinks I was mixing and also the quantity I was consuming. Tequila's were the main culprit. I've reached an age now were my brain can't cope with me mixing drinks anymore. My third holiday I stopped drinking Tequila and I didn't have a single bad day.

On this holiday the only bad day I'd had so far was when I'd had that escapade with my mobile, however I wasn't depressed I was merely pissed off. On January 16th it was complete and utter depression. (This was in the middle of the week spent with Tiger). I had woken up with £2000 in traveller's cheques and 2000 baht in cash and I wasn't due home until March 1st! Even a mingebag Arab couldn't survive with that amount! Actually that's a lie, those cheap cunts could probably get 6 months out there with that. I still hadn't paid for my final month in the hotel and with that realisation the real depression kicked in. It's the first holiday I've had where I've worried about money, it's something that no one should have to do when they're away. It truly is *very* annoying. I was facing a fact that I might have to leave early, which would also mean changing my flight, even more costs. The thought of going home early seemed horrific. I had 13 days left on my visa. Something *had* to be done.

I really didn't want to ask my parents for money as I know they disapprove of my holidays. The only person I could think of who could loan me a decent amount was dealing with his own problems at that time. It was with some hesitation that I contacted him,

'Can you loan me £2000? I'll pay you back £2500 when I come home.'

Before midnight Thai time he'd put the money into my account. The feeling of relief was unbelievable!

The next day I visited a condo block not far from me which sits on Beach Road. I asked to see the two cheapest sea view rooms. Both were cheaper than my hotel and both the rooms were far nicer and bigger than my room. I didn't pay much attention to the rooms though, both times I walked straight to the balcony to look at the view. In both instances the sea view was restricted to a little bit of horizon between high rises. I'm assuming all the rooms at the front of this tower block were privately owned. I made the decision to keep the room I was already in. In fact I'm so happy with my view that I'm just going to carry on paying the extra money and keep this room until the day that I'm thoroughly sick of Soi 7, which may be quite a long way off.

For many years now I've been telling people that if I was offered an all-expenses paid two week holiday to Pattaya I wouldn't accept it. The reason being I'd spend the entire two weeks gutted about having to go back home. On this holiday I realised that my usual 30 day trips will undoubtedly now become a thing of the past. It will have to be a *minimum* of two months from now on. I'm still learning and I'm still changing. I'm not the only thing changing though, that city is starting to become unrecognisable. This was only my second time going there in high season but the difference was huge. The places where girls usually screamed they screamed no longer and Beach Road was incredibly quiet compared to five years previously. Gogo bars disappearing etc. Many men have told me how that city used to be before I ever went there and it sounds like I missed out on a lot. I've got a feeling one day I'll be telling newcomers that they have also missed out on experiences that I got to have. With the current politics of the country the thing that Pattaya is most famous for will eventually be confined to the history books. The day when Soi 7 is torn down and built up as hotels is the day I will, unfortunately, stop going there.

People say that only sex tourists go to Pattaya. I don't think of myself as sex tourist, I prefer to think that I'm more of a selfless missionary going on overseas campaigns to help out people who are less fortunate…I just don't work for free though.

Chapter Twenty-Seven

Hell In Jomtien

If I thought that shopping centre had been an awful experience I was in for a nasty surprise when I had to visit the immigration office in Jomtien.

Luckily the day started with some good fortune for me. I opened the safe to get some cash out, I had a vague memory of an extension visa costing 2000 baht but I took out 3000 just in case I was wrong. I then took out another 1000 baht, unsure of exactly how much a taxi to Jomtien and back costs. So I left my hotel with exactly 4000 baht in my pocket.

This was my first ever visit to Jomtien and it looked very much like Pattaya to me in the daylight. When the taxi was on beach road I couldn't actually see the beach itself, I've always been told it's much cleaner than Pattaya's beach. What I did notice though was that there were no islands to look at. Immediately I made my mind up that Pattaya was better purely for the view of Koh Lan. (Thinking about it now, if the taxi had been heading north maybe you can see that island? I'm not sure)

The taxi pulled up outside the immigration office at around 10:15 and my heart sank when I saw the queue was already outside of the building. When I finally made it inside it was pure bedlam. There was a desk with two poor girls working behind it with tourists coming at them from all sides. The first thing I noticed was that everyone was holding lots of forms in their hands.

What the fuck are these forms?

I'd turned up with nothing but my passport. When I finally got to the desk I explained that I wanted a 30 day extension and the girl handed me two forms, a little card and told me to fill out the forms and get my passport photocopied. After that I entered the main part of the building and the only words that could possibly describe it are 'cattle market'. Everyone shoulder to shoulder and lots of confusion, especially for me. I found a little area to fill out the forms and I couldn't make head or tail of them. Maybe it was because I'd been drinking a litre of whisky a day for nearly two months and I wasn't used to being up so early or maybe it was because those forms literally don't make any sense? I tried my best to fill them out and then I went to the photocopy machine. When the young man working the machine saw that I only had notes on me and not the 7 baht required he took pity and copied my passport for free.

Queuing again I got back to the girl who'd given me the forms, I had people bumping into me the whole time. She looked at the forms, looked at the photocopy and then she pointed to the little card she'd given me. I hadn't bothered reading that card but she placed a finger on a line which read something like 'Proof of residency'. I asked if this was from my hotel. She said yes and told me I couldn't get a visa without it. When I walked out of that building I felt like rolling up into a ball on the floor and crying my eyes out. I don't think I've ever felt stress like it. Just being shoulder to shoulder with people is bad enough but when you don't know what the hell is going on it becomes a living nightmare.

I noticed a raised mini roundabout outside of the building and an old timer sitting on. From sight alone I knew he was English so I walked straight up to him.

'Alright mate, do you know what this proof of residency is all about 'cos I haven't got it.'

'Have you got 4000 baht on you son?'

'Aye, that's everything I have on me.'

'See that woman over there'

He pointed to the left at a set of tables. There was a Thai woman sitting with three tourists.

'Go and give her 4000 baht and tell her you need a stamp. She's been charging people different prices, she charged me 4000 so don't give her any more than that'

I walked to the woman with my 4000 in hand and said to her

'Can you get me a stamp for 4000?'

She took the money, took the forms out of my hand, took my passport and then told me to go and sit down. I went back to the old timer and had a chat with him.

He'd got his stamp over an hour ago from that lady, it had only taken 30 minutes. He advised me to get there just before opening time next time around. He was waiting for his mate who'd refused to pay the extra money, he'd been in there for over an hour and a half.

The lady beckoned me back over and told me to write down my hotel address and room number. She then took me inside a building which looked like a travel agents and took my photo on a mobile. (That little card I'd been given had said that passport photographs were also a requirement) After that I had to go and sit down again. This old timer's mate appeared out from the immigration office in quite a fluster.

'They've knocked me back!'

He had arrived there with a letter from his hotel and receipt of payment for his stay.

'They said they need a more official document!'

The poor lad looked heart broken and if it had been me I definitely would've been broken.

'I'll just come back tomorrow'

The pair of them left. I remember feeling very nervous at this point as I had no proof of residency whatsoever and I wasn't sure if this lady could wangle it. During this time another Englishman had turned up and he was using the same lady as me only she'd charged him 6000 baht and he did have proof of residency!

It seemed to take forever. At one point I asked her how long and she informed me it was going to take a little bit longer to get my stamp, as she explained,

'With you we have to do extra'

This did nothing to settle my nervousness. It took two hours altogether and my poor taxi driver had been sat waiting the whole time. To make up for his lost fares I told him I'd pay double what we'd agreed on once we were back at the hotel.

Next time I go I'll be getting there at 08:30 and I'll be bringing a letter from the hotel. As for those nonsense forms and photographs, the woman sorts all that out for you. There's an easy way and a hard way, easiest ways are always the best in life.

When the taxi was heading back to Pattaya we drove past a traffic accident. Some Westerner had had his front bumper taken off by a baht bus, he must've tried to pull out onto the main road a bit too early. He had a couple of policemen stood next to him and a look of devastation on his face. My taxi driver spoke good English, after passing that crash I said to him,

'That man is lucky. He hasn't just had to go and get a visa'

My opinion of Jomtien after my first ever visit to that town? I fucking hate the place!

Chapter Twenty-Eight

Drugged Up Tigers

I'd had a nice break from Tiger and I'd filled my boots a bit. Once the novelty of being a slag again wore off I decided it was time to go back and see my old friend. When I turned up at the bar she was wearing a bandage from where she'd suffered a sprain. She was clearly in pain, I asked her what the heck she was doing at the bar in that condition. She assured me she was OK, I then asked what painkillers she was on. Blummin' Aspirin! I told her to sit down and stop working and then I headed straight to a pharmacy.

On my walk I remembered a mate telling me that you can buy prescription drugs over the counter in Thailand. I've never taken them in my life, the word 'illegal' has always seemed more appealing to me than 'prescription'. Once I was in the pharmacy I asked the man behind the counter for Valium. I was unsure whether it was a painkiller or not but surely it had to be stronger than Aspirin? Plus I really wanted to try them.

I barfined Tiger, took her to the balcony and we consumed one tablet each. This was the first time that I have ever taken drugs in Thailand. After a time we were both sitting there grinning at each other and feeling incredibly relaxed. I was quite impressed. Once the feeling started to wear off I double-dropped a couple and whilst waiting for them to kick in I decided to take one more. I had absolutely no knowledge of how strong prescription drugs can be. I was pretty away with it once they did kick in. At one point I stood up to change the music on my IPod and I immediately collapsed into the room landing on my face. I had to drag myself across the floor and back up onto the chair. I was absolutely fucked.

It must have been a couple of hours later when Tiger told me she was hungry and going to go out for some food. I was feeling wrecked but I was in a gentlemanly, caring mood for her that night.

'You aren't going anywhere. I'll go and get it'
To be honest I was devastated as it was the last thing I felt like doing. When I walked out of the hotel I was disheartened to see that the food stall which is normally directly outside wasn't there. I had no option but to walk down a busy Soi 7. In my mind I did it walking perfectly straight with my head held high.

The next day when I awoke it was to the sound of Tiger laughing at me. She was holding a packet of little birthday candles.

'Why did you buy these? They're no good'
I laid there scratching my head, probably with a look of confusion on my face. I had no recollection of buying those candles at all! I immediately thought of

the film The Wolf Of Wall Street. There's a scene where the main character is off his tits on Quaalude's and has to drive home from a bar. In his head he thinks he drove home perfectly but he then receives a knock on the door from the police as it turns out he crashed his car numerous times on the way home. I thought of this scene in the film because I wondered to myself if I *had* walked down Soi 7 completely straight with my head held high? I couldn't remember buying those candles at all! Had I in actual fact been stumbling all over the road in a complete state? I will never know the answer.

I spent 6 days with Tiger this time around and Valium was now a daily part of my diet. I found that I quickly built up a tolerance to them. I'd already warned her this would be the maximum length of stay she could have as an old acquaintance of mine was coming over for a week. His arrival was to have a deep impact on my holiday, in the worst of ways and it also soiled the friendship I had built up with Tiger.

Part Four

Sinking Into The Abyss

Chapter Twenty-Nine

Who The Devil Is This Fiend?

There are some people in the world who are *so* pathetic that if you found out they had died you would feel an overwhelming sense of relief. This chapter is about one such individual.

To call him a mate would churn my stomach, I prefer the term 'acquaintance'. We've known each other since we were 11 as we were in the same year at secondary school. If I had to sum him up in one sentence it would probably be something like this....He's as pointless as a midget.

Not too long ago a loose lipped friend of mine told this acquaintance about my books. He bought all three and somehow managed to get through them all. He kindly congratulated me on them via text. The next time I saw him the cock slobbering was unbelievable! It was as if he was talking to a film star! He never actually used the words 'I'm your biggest fan' but I could see in his eyes that's what he wanted me to think. He looked at me in an almost lustful way. The same way a Jew stares at £1 coin.

Before this holiday I'd told him I would be writing a new book and it would definitely be my last one about Thailand. He immediately booked a week's holiday in Pattaya, for no other reason than to be featured in this book. How pathetic is that?! (Admittedly he spent three weeks touring South East Asia before he got here but that was nothing more than a guise to cover his own patheticism)

I told him there was no way I'd be disgracing my book with his real name and asked him to choose a pseudonym. He asked me to call him 'Big Power' which obviously I'm not going to do. I've decided to pick my own name for him, so for the remainder of the book I shall refer to him as 'Savile'.

He maybe a pathetic person but I have to admit we do have quite a bit in common. We're both stubborn, we're both gentlemen but straight talking at the same time and we both have a love of deviancy and intoxication. He outdoes me with some of these traits and I outdo him with the others.

When he arrived it was a day earlier than what I was expecting. What a dampener that put on my day! I waited for him in Tiger's bar and told her she could have the sixth night I'd promised her but I'd be having the afternoon and night with him.

It was early afternoon when I spotted him mincing down Soi 7. I hollered him over. It's always a pleasure sitting with someone you know in Pattaya, regardless of how useless they are. We had a few games of pool and then headed to Soi 6. Savile wanted a ladyboy so it was to a ladyboy bar that we went. He ended up going short time with some bloke,

I wasn't interested, I told him I'd meet him back on Soi 7.

Savile has a few contacts in Pattaya (he's been going there a lot longer than what I have) which means he knows how to purchase a certain illicit drug. In England this drug is common place, I would imagine half of our politicians and royals are putting this stuff up their noses every day. In Thailand however this is a serious crime, dealt with very harshly, which is why I'm not mentioning the drug by name. I think I've given you enough information to guess what I'm talking about though.

On the night time Savile took me to a bar which will remain unnamed, in a certain part of the city which shall also remain unnamed. When we walked in it was full of some of the hardest looking men I've ever seen in my life. One man in particular, when I saw him I thought to myself,

You've definitely murdered at least one person in your life

As is usual with these sorts of hard cases they turned out to be very friendly, personable and jovial. Whilst Savile was sorting out business I was having some interesting conversations and a laugh. Once sorted we headed straight to Savile's hotel which was close by. We enjoyed this certain narcotic and then he also introduced me to Xanax, which he crushed up and we both snorted. He informed me that this could be done with Valium as well.

That night is a blur, the only thing I do remember about it is getting back to my hotel. Tiger was waiting for me, she asked how the night went so I told her what I'd been up to without thinking anything about it. She absolutely hit the roof! Shouting at me whilst she gathered her things. She then stormed out of the room in a right huff. At that point I didn't care less, I don't have time for strait-laced judgemental people. I actually felt a sense of pride because Tiger had informed me many times that no tourist would ever see her get angry. Oops!

There is one good thing I will say about Savile and that's that I admire his stubbornness. It is nearly on a par with my own. Whenever I've made friends in Pattaya they've always ended up just doing the same as me, even to the point of drinking Sangsom and changing their cigarettes to the same as mine. Not so with him, in his week there we had three nights together in total. He wanted to go to his bars and I wanted to go to mine. Neither of us were willing to compromise.

Our last night together we were on Soi 8 playing pool with two Thai's, one a woman and one a ladyboy. Savile took a shine to the woman, the ladyboy was pretty but his behaviour put me off him. Whenever I was lining up a shot he would stand over the pocket exposing his large silicone breasts. This was no sort of behaviour of a gentleman! Plus, if you're going to stick your dick in another man's arse you really have to be in the right mood for it. Savile took them both home in the end. I never asked him what he got up to but I would imagine that at some point they made a meat sandwich with him as the filling. (That's not even a joke by the way, he truly is a deviant.)

When he went home he was as fit as the day he'd arrived. The biggest difference between us is, he doesn't drink much and when it comes to narcotics he has a level of self-control which I just don't possess. He left behind him a complete drug addict. I now consider myself to be a 'Savile victim'.

There you go Christopher, you've got your very own chapter in a Barry J Steel book. Was it worth travelling the 6000 miles you ugly, anal loving homosexual?

Chapter Thirty

The Ten Lost Days

If you start your day by crushing up a Xanax, crushing up a Valium, mixing them together and then snorting the lot then you know you've got a problem. It would take ten days for me to realise that I was doing some serious damage to myself. At the end of those ten days I had a handful of memories and some notes I'd scribbled down. The rest of it was a complete blur, in fact not even a blur, I just had no memory of the vast amount of that period. What I do know is that I was taking large quantities of prescription drugs and also a half decent amount of illegal ones as well. Along with the whisky I basically a mess. (I'd like to quickly point something out to you, never smoke a Thai drug called 'Ice' out there. Its weak, its shit and all it achieves is depriving you of sleep and hunger)

During this period I was mainly having sex with two different people. The stunning ladyboy who'd nearly tricked me. To keep things simple I'll give him a name...Brian will do. He introduced me to Ice but I didn't do it that many times because I thought it was shite. The other person was a proper woman who loved her drugs as well. There were probably others I slept with in that time but they're not in my notes or my memory.

One thing drugs do is make a person filthy, both men and women. Myself and the woman behaved like true animals. I was inserting certain objects inside of her quim and poo-pipe, the manufacturer of these objects would no doubt be appalled if they'd found out. It might possibly have led them to making a disclaimer on the label 'Not to be inserted into sexual orifices'.

I'll tell you about the clear memories that I have from this period. One was standing in that 'gangster bar', a man was talking about his love for Xanax. I flippantly mentioned what I'd been getting up to each day and I remember his face actually dropping. With a very serious look he said to me,

'Mate, stop what you're doing. You're going to kill yourself'
I think I'll remember that moment for a very long time. I didn't listen to him of course.

The three main memories I have were all accidents. The most painful one was when I fell out of the shower. Even before getting in I was a bit wobbly and a little voice in my head was saying,

Have a bath instead
I ignored this voice as I was in a rush to get into bed with that filthy woman. When I fell it was a straight drop. Luckily I broke the fall by slamming the back of

my head on the toilet seat and smashing my right elbow on the floor. The shower curtain was completely intact, it had happened so suddenly that I hadn't even reached out to try and grab anything. It absolutely knacked! I laid on the floor in a moaning, sopping wet mess. The girl had to come in to help me up, dry me down and get me into bed.

The next indecent is probably the most serious of the three. This night I did barfine a different girl but we didn't have chance to have sex. What I remember is sitting on the balcony with my little table in front of me. I was snorting numerous things and I can remember her being very unimpressed with me. After one of the lines I gulped down some whisky to get rid of the taste. I happened to cough when the whisky was in my throat and it spurted back out via my nose and mouth. In this moment I learned that whisky pouring out of your nostrils is incredibly painful, especially if you've been using your nostrils for inappropriate behaviour. I instantly turned into a coughing, wheezing mess. I doubt this impressed that girl either. The next thing I remember is waking up on my front on my bed, I was laid across it sideways with my arms hanging over the edge and I was fully clothed. As I got up I felt like I'd been hit over the back of my head. I immediately checked my pockets, all my money was still there and all my belongings were intact. All I can guess is that I collapsed, hit the back of my head and knocked myself out. I must have put that poor girl through a bit of an ordeal. The position I woke up in led me to believe I had been dragged onto the bed. She couldn't have done that by herself so maybe she got a hotel worker to help, I honestly don't know. No one in the hotel mentioned anything to me about it.

You would think that would've been the straw that broke the camel's back but that incident actually happened about halfway into this little spell of self-destruction. The actual final straw was my last fall. For some reason I decided to headbutt the edge of the dressing table. Maybe it looked at me the wrong way? I put the full weight of my body into the headbutt and afterwards I was laid on the floor. I was conscious and I was in pain with a graze on my forehead. Although the table was unmarked I would like to believe that I won that fight. I wish someone had filmed it, it must have looked spectacular.

The day after that fall I had a long hard look in the mirror. I had grazes on both shins as well as bruises on my arms and legs, with no memory of where they had come from. My brand new phone was covered in cracks and also I'd had to start using Viagra for the first time. Although I always seem to have problems in life, erectile dysfunction has never been one of them. These silly Viagra never seemed to work no matter how many I took, a chubby on was the best I could hope for. One time I became that frustrated with these stupid pills that I started watching porn on my mobile whilst getting piped off. Even that didn't do the trick!

I hadn't come to Pattaya to do any of this stuff. I'd went there to get drunk and have sex like I'd always done. I remembered what that big bloke had said to me and I made the decision to sort myself out. I never touched anymore prescription drugs for the remainder of the holiday. The other stuff I only did two or three more times.

Excess has always been my nature, luckily every now and again a bout of common sense comes along to save me.

Chapter Thirty-One

Cold Turkey With Lashing's Of Ladyboy

If I ever quit something then I end it immediately, I don't believe in weaning. My first night off the drugs I stayed in my room with a 75cl bottle of Sangsom and a woman. It was a jolly old time and I was able to have some proper sex. Earlier on in the night Brian had text me to see what I was up to. I sent back a brief message just saying I was busy.

The whisky did the trick as I fell asleep early that night. It must have been around 03:00 in the morning, I was sound asleep and someone started knocking on my door. At first the knocking became part of my dream but then it became so loud and insistent that it eventually woke me up. It's an understatement to say that I'm quite ratty if someone wakes me up early, even more so when I'm half cut. I was sitting on the edge of my bed putting a pair of shorts on and the knocking was getting louder. As I walked to the door I shouted out,

'Stop *fucking* knocking!'

When I opened it Brian was standing there holding some Ice.

'You need to go home I'm sleeping'

The wally pushed past me and walked straight to the bed and looked at the sleeping woman in it. He then marched into my toilet and locked the door behind himself. I could hear him on his phone speaking Thai in an angry manner. I had no idea what was going on but I felt a sudden urge of anger and started beating on the door. He eventually opened it with tears in his eyes. When I saw the tears I calmed down and politely asked him to leave. Unbeknownst to me the girl in my bed had woken up and was now stood behind me. Bri went straight for her and I grabbed him just in time before he landed a punch on her. He then started shouting death threats at this poor innocent woman, some in Thai and some in English,

'This week you die in motorbike accident!'

If you saw Brian in the flesh you would think he looked like a beautiful woman but what you *have* to remember is that Brian is a man. I'm not a violent person, I have a temper but my bark is worse than my bite. However I was put in a very sticky situation. When I heard the death threat in English instinct kicked in and I pushed him so hard that his feet left the floor and he ended up on his arse in the corridor. With that I slammed the door shut and locked it. My door was then kicked from the other side and I heard some shouting about the Thai police.

It took me a long time to get to sleep after that. I had a terrified girl cuddled into me as if I was some sort of hero but the main thing that kept me awake was the thought of Brian. We'd struck up a good friendship over the last couple of weeks and it was always a pleasure to bum him. I couldn't get the thought of Bri's eyes out my head. When that bathroom door had eventually opened I'd been staring into the eyes of someone who had looked completely and utterly broken. I never want to see a pair of eyes like that again in my life.

The next day I didn't know what to expect. I'd told the girl to go back to her bar and it was probably for the best if I didn't barfine her again, in my mind that was for her own safety. She kept sending me texts, telling me she was thinking of going back home. I was trying to console her saying Brian had just been drunk and jealous and there was nothing to worry about. I told her Bri was angry with me and not her. Truth be told I had absolutely no idea what an angry ladyboy would be capable of, especially one who knows lots of Thai drug dealers.

It was with great joy and relief that I received a very surprising text from Brian at around 14:00. It was an apology! I messaged back and told him it wasn't me he needed to apologise to, it was the girl. I then informed him how terrified this girl was. I received a message back saying he would apologise to her. I phoned the girl up and told her of the offer of an apology but she told me she didn't want any contact with him again. At least it was enough to settle her mind.

I told Bri that it was best if we didn't see each other for a few days as I was still pissed off about the night before, I received a message,

'I understand'

You reach a point where you wonder to yourself if all this type of shit is happening to other men out there or if I just happen to be a magnet for it? Does choosing to be a butterfly mean that you have to expect a certain amount of drama on your holiday? It seems to be part and parcel of all my holidays.

There was one day when I walked past a room close to mine and I could hear a Thai woman screaming at some poor bloke through the door. I pictured him lying on his bed rather gloomily and I thought to myself,

Don't worry mate, I know exactly how you feel

I really feel the need to explain something here. It's strange for me writing about Brian as him/he as he's goddamn beautiful and his company is like that of a woman. In my first book I didn't use those terms but I felt the need to do it in this one. You may have noticed that I'm *slightly* politically incorrect? I strive to fight against political correctness all the time and the current trend these days is a lot of bollocks in our news about 'transgender rights'. It really boil's my piss! A tranny is a bloke with mental issues and it's as simple as that! If they want to act like women then fine it's up to them but they should keep it to themselves and don't bang on about changing certain laws. If they can't keep quiet about it then they should go and see a doctor and ask him for a prognosis on why their brains are so fucked. The day we start taking mentally disabled people seriously is a very sad day indeed.

Please understand that I'm only ranting about Western trannies there, I have no issues with Asian ladyboy's...obviously.

It's a good job that I have absolutely no interest in social media as no doubt I would've been arrested and thrown in prison by now for alleged 'hate speech' (don't even get me started on that law of suppression!). Luckily when it comes to books we do still have a total freedom of speech, how long this will last remains to be seen though.

Chapter Thirty-Two

I Killed A Spider

(No arachnids are harmed in this chapter)

One morning I went to have a wee and when my penis was in my hand I noticed the tip of my foreskin was reddish and swollen. I pulled it back only to find that it was tighter than a Jews wallet. My bellend just didn't look right at all. I poured some hydrogen peroxide onto a cotton bud and started wiping it. Upon contact it stung, which isn't supposed to happen and then whilst wiping it unsightly folds of skin came peeling off my tip. I've had thrush before, I knew exactly what I was dealing with. I only had one concern though, I went onto google to find out if you can catch it from oral sex, luckily the answer was yes.

I started wracking my brain to think of who I'd been with in the last few nights. It was a complete blur. Obviously the damage caused during my prescription drug habit still hadn't fully healed. The only memory I had was a girl who'd been piping me off and when doing so she'd been scraping her teeth on my glans. I'd asked her numerous times to stop doing this but the sadist had completely ignored me until I'd had to shout at her. I was left in no doubt that this was the culprit who'd given me my first STD in many a year. The only problem was I couldn't remember her face or which bar I'd gotten her from. All I could remember were those evil teeth. If I had been able to remember these two things I would've had no qualms about approaching her and having a very discreet, quiet word in her ear. It's every man's duty.

I had thrush around three or four times in my younger days and I remembered it only took 24 hours to clear using Canesten Cream. When I visited the pharmacy I made the mistake of buying the cheaper Thai stuff. The next day my willy looked exactly the same so I went back and bought the real stuff. Another blummin 48 hours for even that to work! It must have been super thrush for it to take three goddamn days to heal. That's the longest I went without having sex this holiday. A dose of thrush isn't going to put me off unsheathed blowjobs but I'm always going to remain very wary of these toothy women. (I should hasten to add that I meant *receiving* blowjobs in that line)

During my three days of abstinence all I could do was drink. My days of having one night off the booze each week had stopped at some point in January. During my daily afternoon ritual of drinking a 35cl bottle of Sangsom before going out I'd decided to stop putting water in it as I'd started finishing the bottle far too quickly. I was now drinking hardcore every single night.

During my drug phase I'd lost my appetite, I'd been forcing a bowl of krapow moo into myself daily. (A lovely dish by the way) When I'd knocked the drugs on the head my appetite never returned, I was still living on one bowl of food a day. On a couple of days I couldn't even do that, I'd had to force a Snickers Bar down me before drinking.

By now I'd blown all my money again, I'd asked my brother for money and eventually caved in and ended up asking my parents for money as well. I was now in debt to the tune of £4000. Hiding my money from myself had been the wisest decision of my life, I dread to think how much of it I would've spent if it had been available to me. My biggest error though was emptying my account and going over there with nothing but an overdraft as backup. I will never make this same stupid mistake ever again.

I was telling myself at the time that three months was too long for me. Looking back now I can see that isn't true, if I'd just stuck to whisky I would've been fine. But I hadn't just stuck to whisky though, my actions during the first half of February had left me wiped out both mentally and physically. Now I was just a borderline alcoholic mess of a man. Even the pleasure of ejaculation had been taken from me, if I was drunk having sex it just wasn't happening no matter how long I went for. For that pleasure I now had to be sober.

I made a decision during this period that I'm actually going to stick to. I realised that I couldn't do five straight months out there, my lack of self-control would be the end of me. A wiser choice would be to split my holiday into two, a two month holiday and a three month holiday with a month or two in between them. This would also mean I'd avoid having to do the dreaded border run, something I have yet to do. My only problem with this plan is figuring out which months will best to avoid the Songkran Festival and also be available for work. I'm sure you'll agree that in the scheme of things, this is a very good problem for anyone in the world to have.

Chapter Thirty-Three

Some Overdue Muck

7 nights left. On this particular night I was walking past a bar and a girl shouted me over. Her height and figure ticked the right boxes but she had an incredibly innocent face. I noticed that she had a couple of tattoos in naughty places so I told myself there was probably a little demon behind those angelic looks. We got chatting and I asked her how old she was, when she told me she was 32 I felt like biting my knuckles. It really is quite annoying at how well preserved these people are!

I bought her a drink and sat with her. When she asked if we could go back to my room after this drink my suspicions about her being dirty were confirmed. It was only just after 22:30. Gee whiz did I underestimate how dirty this girl would turn out to be! By far the dirtiest Thai woman I've ever had, even putting Tiger to shame. I've decided to name this girl Filth, which may seem a bit disrespectful but by the end of this chapter you will agree with me that the nickname is very apt.

We had sex pretty much straight away and during that first session I realised she was game for it. We were sitting on my balcony afterwards and she asked if she could give me a blowjob. It's probably the stupidest question I've ever been asked in my entire life. After whipping down my shorts she got on with it whilst I was smoking a fag. After a time she lifted my legs up and beckoned me to shift to the edge of the seat. The feeling of getting your bumhole licked whilst smoking is a little bit terrific. The only downside was the uncomfortable position I was in. I must have looked like a disabled person from Soi 7.

During our second session in the bedroom I learned that she liked to be spanked. Yet again this was another girl who asked me to hit her. I must have been in a semi-conscious state by the end of that session because when I went in the bathroom afterwards I had an unpleasant surprise waiting for me. The nasty pasty had given me eight love bites! One big one on each side of my neck and the rest were spread across my collar bones. I immediately shouted,

'Oi you! Get in 'ere!'

When she stood in the doorway and asked me what was wrong. I replied,

'What the fuck are all these?'

She let out a giggle.

'No one else will want you now. You are mine for the next 6 days'

'Well I'm going to piss on you for doing that to me'

She let out another giggle,

'OK, you can do'

And so I pissed on a woman for the first time in my life. It took me about five minutes of straining with the tap running before it sprayed out of my Japs eye. The spoil sport wouldn't let me piss on her face or in her mouth so I was limited to her tits. Enjoyable.

It's worth pointing out that I wasn't going to let myself be accosted in such an unsporting fashion. I didn't keep her for the remainder of my trip but I did go back to her for the majority of it.

She was yet another girl with a foreign boyfriend. Each morning she would go and sit in my bathroom at a certain time for the ritual phone call. I could never hear him, only her. I'm assuming it was always video calls because the first call I heard her say,

'I'm at my friends, she's not well'

You would think that video calls would've put an end to bargirl mischief but it turns out that these men are so blind in love that they believe anything that they're told! (I'll give you a tip men. When video calling, if you don't recognise the background then ask her to turn her phone around and walk into main room. If it turns out to be me laid there then I profusely apologise)

From these calls I gathered that he was a deeply needy and insecure man. She seemed to spend the full twenty minutes of each call reassuring him about different things. Typical lines would be,

'OK my love, I'm sure things will be fine'

'Don't worry my love, your boss will be OK'

Sometimes I couldn't help but shake my head whilst listening to her. I remember after the very first call when she came back into my bed I'd said to her,

'I'm sure your boyfriend is a lovely man, but he's a fucking idiot'

I have actually had a change of heart about bargirls. The pessimist in me has always believed that they never actually fall love. I don't believe that's true anymore but what I will say is that, for a lot of them, their version of love isn't the same as *normal* love. For a bargirl it's the same type of love that English ten year olds have in a school playground.

One night I was sitting with her and she'd been drinking Singha. On the little table in front of us were two empty bottles, one small one large. I pointed to the smaller bottle and said,

'Can I put that in you?'

She pointed at the bigger bottle,

'Why not that one? Why not your hand?'

'You want me to fist you? Have you been fisted before?'

'Yes, in my pussy and my ass'

It really pains me to write 'ass' instead of 'arse' but that's how she said it. When we went for it I used an incredible amount of lube. I don't know who'd fisted her before, either a woman or a man with very small hands but I just couldn't get my thumb knuckle in. Everything else was in except for this one pesky knuckle. I tried three times and she let out a scream each time, I had to give up in the end. I couldn't fault her for trying though. Afterwards she had a big sore gash that resembled a sight from the scene of a crime, unable to use it I decided to sit on her face with my balls in her mouth and wanked myself off. It was the first time that I came whilst drunk in a long time and it was in her mouth. Naturally she swallowed it.

My only regret with my time spent with her was when she'd asked if her friend could come over. My last threesome had been a complete waste of money so I declined the offer. Looking back now I know she would've put a lot more effort in than the last two.

Now you know why her name is Filth.

Chapter Thirty-Four

Deep Sigh

A man's penultimate night in Pattaya is always better than his last night. Last nights are generally a miserable affair. It was the other way around for me this time.

On my penultimate night I took Filth to my favourite bar to meet my friend. I class this woman as a genuine mate and I've known her for years now. She's not the prettiest of women and she's very overweight but she speaks impeccable English and is really funny. This description of her is something I always tell the bargirls if I ever mention her. However this information, along with the fact that I've never slept with her, never seems to stop girls who I barfine getting jealous of her. I learned very quickly with Filth that she was a *very* jealous woman.

I was sitting having a laugh with my mate and Filth just sat there with a face like thunder not speaking a word. After a while it really began to piss me off. I'd already asked her what was wrong a few times but now I'd got to the point where I felt like she was spoiling my night.

'You aren't coming out with me tonight. You can either go to my room and wait for me or you can go back to your bar and find someone else'

'No, I'm coming out with you'

'No you're not'

'OK I go back to my bar'

'You can keep the barfine'

With that she stormed off. I did a circuit of my favourite bars and I spotted a girl who I'd barfined a couple of times early on in the holiday. She acted very pissed off with me. In turn this pissed me off. I hate people getting angry with me for no reason. I'm always upfront with every girl about being a butterfly. You would think they would just be happy for the money? Two angry women was enough to put a bit of a dampener on the night.

On my final night I was absolutely smashed. I was sitting with my mate and I told her that I was ready to go home. I have never once said that on any previous holidays. Normally I'll just sit at bars looking miserable and feeling sorry for myself. This night I was happy, laughing and joking without a care in the world. I didn't even barfine anyone at the end of the night. Everything changed the next morning though. God I was miserable! That day I told myself that I probably could've done another month out there.

I'll give you a top tip that I do every holiday now. I book the 01:30/02:30 flight on the day *after* my visa runs out. As long as I pass through immigration before midnight it's OK. This means you get the full last day. Usually my last day is spent in my room having sex and being consoled. On this last day I was in my room alone. I received three text messages, from Tiger, Filth and Brian. (I forgot to mention that I was back in touch with Tiger. I'd went to see her after I quit the drugs. I'd pop into her bar every other night to buy her a drink and have a chat and we were also texting each other. I never barfined her though as I didn't want to risk falling out with her again).

When I received these messages I wished them all well and told them I wasn't in the mood for company. In the afternoon I packed my suitcase and went out drinking.

When the taxi came I was pretty drunk and I fell asleep almost immediately. I was having a very vivid dream about drinking on Soi 7 when the taxi driver woke me up. In a minor state of confusion I looked at the driver and then at the airport outside of the window. I could've cried! To be sat in a bar, in my mind, only to realise that I was actually at the airport was one of the most disheartening experiences I've ever had. I was no longer pissed now, just pissed off. The massive queues I had to stand in didn't help either.

When I pass through immigration the miserable officers usually make a point of staring at their watch and then giving me a snotty look. The one this time was OK, he looked at my passport and let out a grin.

'Your last night eh?'

I managed to smile back, just an empty smile though. For the entire flight home all I could think about was my pot of money and a return ticket.

What do you make of a man who spent an entire three months living on Soi 7 without feeling the need to venture out to other wonderful places? I'm thinking about starting up a petition to put pressure on the Thai government to change the name of Soi 7 to Soi Barry. I'd also make a demand that I want a solid gold statue of me erecting in the middle of the street. Hopefully this will be enough for them to say,

'OK, OK! You can have the name change but *not* the statue'

Chapter Thirty-Five

I'm Not A Complete Mongoloid

I had left England during a blizzard and I returned during the worst blizzard the country had had in decades. No one back home had bothered to warn me about this.

When I stepped out of Newcastle Airport it was probably the happiest and most joyous moment of my entire life…it was freezing cold, snow was blowing in my face, I was unemployed and homeless. If a moving vehicle had been passing in front of me at that moment in time I probably would've stepped in front of it and ended it all there and then. Luckily there wasn't one so I walked to the taxi rank dragging my suitcase behind me with my head down to keep the snow out of my face. The taxi driver was a jolly man, I really couldn't be arsed with him.

That full first day was utter depression. Fortunately I had a list of chores to sort out and I started them the very next day. This gave me something to focus on. After three days the chores were complete and I'd adjusted back to normal life. I then started my countryside walks again. This was something I did everyday regardless of the weather. Admittedly during the first week I would spend the majority of my walks panting like a Nigerian rapist.

A person reading this book may be forgiven for believing that I'm a raging alcoholic on a path to self-destruction. I can assure you that I can be very sensible when required to be. What you have to remember about me is that I didn't let an ex-wife get the better of me, I didn't let unemployment beat me, I didn't let drugs beat me and I will certainly never let alcohol get the better of me. Normally after a 30 day holiday I have a minimum of one week off the booze but after this holiday I told myself I needed at least one month off it. Apart from nicotine I went full on cold turkey.

You would think that going from one extreme to another would put your body into shock? Surprisingly I was ok, there were no shakes or cravings at all. The only two side effects were rapid weight loss and not being able to sleep properly. I didn't actually get a decent nights kip until my sixteenth night back, up until then I'd been averaging 4 hours a night. Before the holiday I'd weighed 178lbs, which according to the BMI scale is my ideal weight...if you believe in that type of shite. When I came home I'd put on 13lbs. By rights it should've been more, I'm confident I lost weight during my final month due to my horrific lifestyle at the time.

After 3 weeks at home, walking every day and not drinking, I'd lost 15lbs! It's amazing how cutting out a liquid can affect your metabolism. It was also after 3 weeks that I got back offshore, this would secure me another 3 weeks off the drink. One of the many perks of my job is that my liver is guaranteed a rest. Altogether I was off the drink for six weeks and four days. Feel free to have a go of doing that.

When I was back at work I had to remember how to do my job again. Anything involving straight lines I found especially difficult. In the three weeks before this job I'd been concentrating on finding employment, my evil plan and also typing up this shit. Once surrounded by sea again all I could think of was Pattaya and how long it was going to take to get back there.

I'd had to buy a new phone once I was home. I decided, against my better judgement, to stay in touch with Filth and Tiger. I only lasted four days with Filth before I had to block her. She expected constant video calls! Along with Islam, I think video calls are the worst man made invention ever! Surely only controlling deviant minds could've came up with both of those *disgusting* ideas?

I would get the same texts from her every night,
'I want to see you'
'No, I'm with my parents'
'You with lady!'

Bearing in mind she's a hooker with an Australian boyfriend! The couple of video calls we did have I barely got to see her anyway. She would have the phone pointed at her mates which meant I found myself staring at strangers. One call I found myself face to face with a couple of blatantly gay Thai men! Enough was enough so I blocked her. I've kept her number for when I go back though. Me and her have some unfinished business which may or may not involve my right hand and a tube of lube.

I'm still currently in touch with Tiger but even with her things have started to change. Her messages are getting more serious these days. One example was this,

'I don't know how I will feel when I see you with other women again'

This basically means I'm almost certainly guaranteeing myself more drama when I do go back. One thing is for certain, I will be putting a big candle in my suitcase and I intend to use it well before she falls out with me.

Chapter Thirty-Six

The Evil Plan: Part Two

The day I concocted my evil plan was also the day I knew I would be writing a new book. The original book I planned was quite different from the one in your hands though. It was to be called Getting Off The Grid. It was going to be split into three parts, part one similar to part one of this book only more detailed. Part two would've been about my holiday and part three about living in my motorhome. When the time came close for me to start writing it I had a change of heart. I knew that title would attract Green Peace weirdo's and the like, who would've been absolutely appalled by the content. When I came up with the title Thailand Ting Tong I knew it was a keeper, but I couldn't write a book with 'Thailand' in the title and only have a third of it set in that country. So I came up with a new plan...write this book and also a companion book called 'Barry J Steel Came In A Motorhome'. That second book is getting scrapped now (read the next chapter for an explanation). This brief chapter is replacing that book.

When I got home I had a very specific van and budget in mind. I'd never driven a large vehicle in my life and wary of jumping in at the deep end I wanted a smaller model. I would have to wait until May 2018 before I purchased my new 'home'. By then I was 37 years old and officially semi-retired!

I had it delivered very late in the day and due to slightly high alcohol levels in my system it meant I couldn't drive it that night. There were numerous things I had to buy for it before it could be considered habitable anyway. At one point in that night I went and sat in it for half an hour whilst heavily drunk. I felt incredibly happy sitting there fantasising about where I could be. After that night a very strange feeling came over me, it was one of mild fear. I wasn't scared of driving it and I wasn't scared of sleeping in it. It's hard to describe exactly how I felt but I suppose the fear could be summed up in this line,

'This is it now, I hope I'm going to like it?'

It sat there on my mams driveway a few days before I actually took out. I know that sounds stupid and thinking back now I don't understand why I was like that. When I did eventually drive it one of the first things I realised was that I would no longer be able to take corners and roundabouts in the manner in which I was accustomed. Any fears of driving a bigger vehicle diminished when I realised that the higher up you are the easier it is to drive.

I have a very long list of places I want visit on this little island of ours. The top spots are the west coast of Scotland, Devon and Cornwall. Basically all the places where I could never afford to live. For my first adventure though I thought I'd try somewhere close to home that I'm familiar with so I chose the Lake District. To get there I had to drive over one of England's most scenic and also dangerous roads, the A66. I think I know one of the reasons that road has such a high fatality rate. At one point you have to drive past a group of camels! It's hard *not* to take your eyes off the road when there's the bizarre sight of camels roaming around the English countryside. I think I might need to go and get my eyes tested because as I drove past them I noticed a road sign. At first glance I thought it read 'All Arab Visitors MUST Wear Chastity Belts!' Upon closer inspection though I realised it simply said 'Mainsgill Farm'.

The feeling I had driving along that road was one of ecstasy. Complete freedom! Singing Peter Gabriel's Sledgehammer at the top of my lungs (and murmuring the lines I didn't know). Liberation! No more council tax and the sweetest one of all, a TV without a license.

What a satisfying feeling it is to get one over on that paedophile haven known as the BBC!

I'd thought about packing a bottle of whisky for the trip but then I thought better of it. Not for any fear of driving over the limit, an altogether different reason. I'm going to tell you a fact that you might not know. In our national parks camping outside of designated sites is technically illegal! If a jobsworth park ranger tells you to move then you have to, if you refuse then the police are called! It's ridiculous! If the police arrive and you're drunk then you're pretty much fucked as it's classed as being drunk whilst in charge of a vehicle. Obviously if you hand over your cash and stay on a boring campsite then suddenly it's perfectly fine to have a drink! And then there's that other strange anomaly, if you happen to be a filthy pikey then you can do whatever you want. They get the same immunity from British police as Muslim pedos! Strangely enough the most draconian country in Britain, Scotland, doesn't have any camping laws. You can park up wherever you want and get smashed without fear of being moved.

When I got to the Lakes I found a perfect spot on Ullswater. I parked up and put the kettle on. I made myself a nice cup of Options mint flavoured hot chocolate. Yes that's right, the £4 stuff, I don't fuck about.

(It was on offer for £2.50 in Tesco) After that I sat by the lake smoking and listening to music. It was lovely but a drink would've made it even better though. The view I had was the south end of Ullswater, undoubtedly one of the best views in the whole of England and it was a perfect sunny evening. As the sun went down shadows climbed slowly up the mountain sides until it engulfed them. Casanova 70 by Air came on in my headphones. A special moment for me was that.

I'd gone to the Lakes demanding an actual lake view. To get it meant parking in a layby on the road. This position left me certain that a ranger would pull up at some point and tell me to move. By night time no one had come. I took out my newly purchased thermals for sleeping in but when I took them out of the packaging was horrified to discover that my white T-shirt was actually a white sleeveless vest! It made me look incredibly camp! I was no longer bothered about a ranger asking me to move, now I was just afraid of a ranger seeing me in that gay vest! Putting that thought out of my mind I decided to christen the van by having quite a furious wank in it. I could feel the whole vehicle rocking during it!

In the morning I woke up early to catch the sunrise. There wasn't a cloud in the sky and the lake was as calm as millpond. I sat there and enjoyed my morning cuppa. At that moment in time there wasn't anywhere else on Earth that I would rather have been. Sitting there with that view I knew I'd made the right decision. This was the life that I was *supposed* to have. It's worth noting that on that very same morning, whilst I was sitting on the shores of Ullswater, a certain American lady was sitting in Windsor waiting to get married.

My life is a mixture of three extremes. In my private life I want complete solitude, in my working life I have to live in the middle of the sea with my work colleagues and then there's my Pattaya life. Right now the mixture of these 3 extremes is perfectly balanced. There's not one of these lives I could single out and live all year round, I don't even think there are even two I could mix and live all year round. I need all three of them and I can only hope the balance remains the same as long as possible. My working life is unfortunately the most important of the three as it dictates the other two. That's the same sad truth for everyone on this planet though.

No one believed me when I told them what I was going to do. When I put my house on the market there was shock within my family but I still don't think they believed that I was actually going to go through with it. People have a tendency to project their own fears of something onto you. Thank Allah I don't share these same fears. I was a man who had absolutely nothing to lose.

P.S

I wish I'd kept those stupid pedestal bin bags as they'd have come in handy in my van!

Chapter Thirty-Seven

RIP Barry J Steel

When I'm with my mates, as a joke, I refer to my pseudonym in the third person. For instance I might say something like,

'I wonder what Barry Steel would do in this situation?'

Although Barry is me, I see him almost like a separate character as he is purely the dark side of my personality. Very few of my redeeming qualities feature in my books. You will just have to take my word for it that I do possess some. My mates also play along and speak about him as if he is some other person. I've got a feeling that a couple of them actually prefer Barry to me!

There was just over a year period where this monster completely took over my life and I thoroughly enjoyed every single minute of it. The writing seemed to flow back then. This is now my fourth book and as with all my past hobbies I've grown thoroughly bored of it. What a blummin chore this has been for me to get it finished! I hate doing things that I have no interest in! I *had* to write this though because it is the single most interesting thing that I have ever done in my life. There will come a time in the future when I'm grey and old and I will read this with a smile on my face. (Or feel thoroughly ashamed of myself?)

I suppose I should take this opportunity to apologise for the shortness of this book. It could've been longer. When it came to typing up all my scribbling's there were some stories I threw away because they were too similar to things I'd written before and also some of them were just plain boring wank. I also had some pages I must've written when I was blind drunk because it literally looked like it had been written in Arabic! I had absolutely no idea what it said! My handwriting is as bad as a doctors when I'm sober never mind when I'm pissed. For me the shortness of the book is a sure sign that I've ran out of things to say.

My second book was a sort of mini autobiography but the other two and this one have chronologically catalogued a six year period of my life. Undoubtedly the most interesting years of my life so far. The position I'm in right now means that my life is surely destined to become more interesting. As for Barry J Steel though, I'm afraid it's the end of the road for him. (Did I just hear you breathe a sigh of relief?!).

I suppose this is good news for those people who read my books just to make themselves feel angry. Deep down those left-wing fascists probably have a little feeling of disappointment. To lose a source of anger can't be very good for people whose lives seem to thrive on being angry. I have a question for you. Could you ever finish a book that you thought was completely shit? I know I definitely couldn't.

A man once said,
    'Never say never'
Dr Frankenstein resurrected his monster a fair few times so one day I might resurrect mine. For the foreseeable future though Barry is dead.

Chapter Thirty-Eight

My End

I realise that with this book I have created a work of disgusting filth. I think the only taboo I haven't covered is necrophilia. Would I ever fuck a corpse? Probably not. That's that one covered now.

I'm interested in knowing how a person feels after reading something like this? Are you a hardcore Pattaya addict, who wasn't expecting to be reading about pedestal bins and solstices? Are you someone who has never been to Pattaya and wasn't expecting to read about explicit gay sex? Do you have a vagina instead of a penis? There are *so* many questions I would love to ask.

Do you intend to use this book to wipe your mucky arsehole with? (If you're reading this on a kindle then I would advise against doing this) If you intend to keep hold of your copy where will you keep it? Hidden out of sight or proudly on your bookshelf? Will you discuss this with a friend/work colleague or will it be your dirty little secret?

I will never find out the answers to these questions, such is the nature of writing books using a pseudonym. All I can say right now is that it's been a pleasure for me to spend time in your company. Now it's time for you to stop reading about my life and go out and enjoy your own. I really hope that you have a long and fruitful one. (I'm talking about your life there *not* your willy)

Dear reader, I would like to leave you with one little piece of advice if I may? In the remainder of your short existence on this planet please don't do anything that I wouldn't do. And I mean that very sincerely by the way. Definitely, definitely *don't* do *anything* that I wouldn't do!

The End

ALL PROCEEDS FROM THIS BOOK ARE
DONATED TO THE BARRY JUDAS STEEL
FUND FOR THAI WOMEN IN NEED

Made in the USA
Las Vegas, NV
21 February 2022

44361732R00095